MW00883783

FOLLIS: GREATNESS
TRANSCENDS

Ralph N. Paulk & Herman D. Smith

Published by the Charles Follis Foundation, 2023.

FOLLIS: GREATNESS TRANSCENDS

First edition. September 8, 2023

Printed in the United States of America
Editor: Travis Moran
Publisher: Charles Follis Foundation
www.CharlesFollis.org

INTRODUCTION

Space for Greatness

◆ ◆ ◆

The Romans, it is true, had at the time a football game of their own which was called **"Follis".**

There was no limitation upon the number of players, but these were equally divided between two sides. The ball was passed forward by a man standing at midfield and the game was in action. The object being to drive the ball by passing, kicking, or carrying across the opposite goal-line. Its progress was impeded by blocking, holding, and tackling. But here the similarity to Rugby ends, as this ancient game was a prolonged scrimmage without order or method. When the Romans came in contact with the Greeks and seized their novel and admirable institutions, they also adopted this game, slightly Latinizing the name to "harpastum." —Parke Hill Davis, *Football: the American Intercollegiate Game*

Why does the Pro Football Hall of Fame lack a bronze bust of Charles Walter Follis?

After all, Follis is the Jackie Robinson of professional football—or rather Robinson became the Charles Follis of Major League Baseball. Coincidentally, Branch Rickey, who helped Robinson break baseball's color barrier in 1947, was even Follis' backfield backup and occasional roommate with Shelby Athletic Association in 1902. Follis was also considered one of the best baseball players in the country: In 1906, only months after being forced into retirement from football, he signed with the Cuban Giants of the Negro Baseball League. In a different world, Follis easily could have become the first Black man to play professional baseball, too.

Dreaming of becoming one of MLB's first Black players, Follis once left his home in Wooster, Ohio, for Chicago, hoping to convince the Cubs that he was too exceptional for them to slam the door in his face. The Cubs, who had heard of the mercurial Follis, took one look at him, then promptly banished him from the grounds. There were even threats to throw him in jail for trespassing. If anything, he could have been charged with having the audacity to believe that he was the white man's equal—if not better.

Like Robinson, Follis was also a staunch advocate for Black rights. In 1909, Follis was helping spread the message of W. E. B. DuBois, who founded the National Association for the Advancement of Colored People just over a year before Follis' controversial death on April 5, 1910, at the age of 31. Follis had garnered a great deal of attention, and his presence troubled some in the community, partly because he was actively involved with political causes, issues that focused on the advancement of Black people.

If only he had been as outspoken as heavyweight champion Jack Johnson for whom he develops a mostly long-distance friendship. Johnson was beginning his trek toward the title at the same time that Charles was building the football program at Wooster in 1898. In 1903, while Charles is high-stepping in Shelby, Johnson survives a 20-round bout with "Denver Ed" Martin to win the World Colored Heavyweight championship. Charles' niece, Laura Hood Jackson, recalls her mother telling the story of how he was in awe of Johnson. Eventually, the two developed a mutual respect. Their paths would cross often enough that they agreed to meet in exhibition matches or sparring sessions. Charles and Johnson admired each other, partly because of their shared struggles as Black athletes. Each man was determined to prove that Black men, when given the opportunity, could shatter the myth of the superior white athlete. When Johnson destroys Jim Jeffries in 1910, all hell breaks loose as race riots occur all across America. Blacks celebrated Johnson's historic victory as one for racial advancement, if not atonement. Around the country, Blacks hold spontaneous parades and gather in prayer meetings. Black poet William Waring Cuney later noted this Black reaction to the fight in his poem, "My Lord, What a Morning." Blacks celebrated similarly in Wooster when Charles made his debut with the Shelby Athletic Association nearly eight years earlier.

Even after his suspicious death, Follis continued to have a remarkable impact on American culture. By thriving amid racism and violence, he broke through walls for the likes of Hall of Famer Marion Motley, who in 1946 would become the first Black player in the NFL—but also for a long line of legendary Black running backs.

And yet, while these reasons are all valid, another transcends them all: One could argue that the very business model of professional football is based on Charles Follis. Before he came along, the pre-NFL leagues were mired in the muck and struggling to generate fan interest beyond the local level. Suddenly, a 6-foot, 200-pound prototype halfback was giving even the most hostile fans something to cheer about and, ironically, someone to hate.

No official tally of Follis' total yards or even total touchdowns from his Shelby years exists. Statistics from the era are iffy at best. What we do know is that he had 11 runs over 70 yards in the 1902 season—an unmatched number in any era. And even that number would have been greater had he been able to finish long runs without being blindsided by interceding fans.

Soon, however, every football franchise owner began to realize that ticket and refreshment sales—plus overall community and business participation—would skyrocket whenever "Follis The Speedy" rolled into town. His presence enabled owners to record their highest earnings, thus setting the stage for what ultimately would become the NFL draft—an assembly line of talented football players. It's a system designed to discover the next Charles Follis.

In many respects, Charles was among the first free agents as well; nearly every franchise in pro football's infancy tried to lure him from Shelby with better wages. This phenomenon caused owners across the league to start hiring ringers or paid all-stars to play in big games to match Charles' unparalleled athleticism. His superior play showed owners the many benefits of having such a magnetizing individual on their team and allowed them to amass generational wealth and political influence.

Follis faced greater obstacles to success in this extraordinarily brutal era. The game would become exceedingly fatal during his time. In 1904, at least 18 deaths and 159 serious injuries, mostly among high schoolers, are reported as a result of football. Today, NFL players would be banned for several games—if not entire seasons—for committing the flagrant roughing violations heaped upon Charles Follis. He was spiked, kicked, punched, bitten, eye-gouged, cursed, spat upon, and called *nigger* more often than anyone wants to remember. Teammates respected Follis for his tenacity, but also for his awe-inspiring grace. He could have retaliated, but he was able to march into history with his dignity intact—and he would discover that his work as a Black rights activist was more meaningful than his marvels on the gridiron.

Follis was football's first real *impact player*—that

indescribable athlete who teams feared to play and fans flocked to see. He cleared every hurdle—defenders, overzealous fans, and hate—to establish a reputation steeped in secrecy because of the color of his skin. Without Follis, we may never have seen the NFL become a trillion-dollar juggernaut with unmatched social and political sway among America's sports.

"The next step is the Hall of Fame," proclaimed Follis' late great-grandniece Lydia Thompson, who led a successful effort to rename the Wooster High School football field in 1994. She had grown up in the town's Black community, where stories of Charles Follis were shared by his relatives and others who remembered him:

To be part of history is exciting. To create history is extraordinary. ... We want to be part of, not apart from, the community. I knew Charles' brother Joe. I knew Charles' nieces, I knew his sister-in-law, and Mrs. Follis shared the story with us. I love history, I love remembering, and if someone has done something that impacts the community, the community should be willing to give back by honoring that person. It's been over a century since Charles raced off into history. Those of you who cherish history ... who respect history, give Charlie his due. This is an honor long overdue.

She closed with these words: "Run on Charles, you belong to the ages."

Thompson launched a campaign to get her great-grand uncle inducted, convincing the Wooster City

Council to adopt an informal resolution asking the Hall to honor Follis.

Don Smith, then vice president of public relations at the Hall of Fame, responded that the hall's administration has "no say in who gets in."

"We will certainly run (Follis) by the board of selectors," Smith said, but he cautioned, "Most likely, his contributions wouldn't be enough to get into the Hall of Fame. We do recognize his role in history as the first Black to sign a professional contract."

A nominee must receive 80 percent approval to be elected to the Pro Football Hall of Fame. The current Selection Committee comprises 49 members (just six of whom are Black); from that group, 12 are selected to serve as a Seniors Committee. Today, that committee is the *only* obstacle remaining between Charles Follis and his rightful place in the Pro Football Hall of Fame.

It's unlikely Follis himself would have made any fuss about his exclusion. For much of his five years in pro football, the three-sport star excelled in anonymity. The then-white-only media in Ohio, who cares very little about what Follis *thinks*, never interviews him.

Though his impact has yet to resonate with mainstream media, Follis' impact on the path of professional football cannot be understated.

In 1975, the *Akron Beacon Journal* launched an informal campaign to get Charles Follis enshrined after writer John Seaburn discovered Follis had signed a contract with the Shelby Blues in 1904. Also in 1975, as Wooster celebrated being named an All-American City with a civic gala and parade, relatives of the original Follis family were seated proudly on a float, smiling and remembering America's first but forgotten Black professional sports superstar. Now, nearly 50 years later, momentum is building again.

Ironically, Follis' accomplishments have been recognized all around Ohio:

- In 1976, he was inducted into the Wayne County Hall of Fame.
- In 1989, he was inducted into the Wooster High School Hall of Fame.
- In 1998, the high school renamed its football stadium Follis Field to honor him.
- In 2018, Governor John Kasich signed legislation designating February 3 as "Charles Follis Day" to honor the first African-American professional football player.

And in 2019, Shelby—a city with only 16 African Americans—dedicated a street in his honor. "Charles Follis Way" is located only a few blocks from the stadium in which he made his professional debut. Ironically, in Follis' time, Shelby was known as a "sundown town," meaning Blacks were not permitted to be in public after sunset. Shelby was a city designed to keep Black Americans out, and yet Charles Follis closed the cultural divide with his otherworldly performances and his dignified character. Over a century after his death, such an honor proves how far Follis' influence extended beyond sports.

Sandra Smith and Dawn Smith descendants of Charles Follis with Shelby city officials (Joe Gies and Mayor Steven Schag) for "Charles Follis Way" street dedication in 2020.

In the Hall of Fame today, there is a five-by-seven photo of Charles Follis alongside others of several Blacks who also played professional football before the National

Football League was founded in 1920. If you ask players today if they've ever heard of Charles Follis, most have no clue, and assert that it was Motley who broke football's color barrier.

One has to ask: "Why is the NFL reluctant to acknowledge the 'pre-NFL' pioneers of professional football?"

Follis was the catalyst that made the pro football's early successes possible. Indeed, he was its original game plan. The league was mired in controversy before Follis arrived, losing the support of its communities and catching the rebuke of lawmakers. It was hemorrhaging money, and the burgeoning sport of baseball was usurping the general public's interest. Prior to Follis' arrival in Shelby, stadiums could barely sell 200 tickets; suddenly they were selling 2,500—leaving standing room only to see this Black marvel perform. The thought of having a Charles Follis on every team excited ownership to capitalize on his athletic abilities and the pure excitement he brought to the game.

When Follis retired from professional football in 1906, his vacancy was filled by Charles "Doc" Baker, the *second* Black pro football player, who played two years as a running back with the Akron Indians. After Baker, there was Henry McDonald, who had a six-year career as a running back with the Rochester Jeffersons. Then Robert "Rube" Marshall would play tight end for the Rock Island Independents. Frederick "Fritz" Pollard would become the first Black professional head coach when Akron signed him in 1920. After the NFL formed in 1920, a few Blacks were allowed to play, thus creating more revenue and a frenzied following. However, the old prejudices of those in charge soon resurfaced. Blacks were banned from 1933 to 1946. Why? For the very reasons those in charge discriminate against minorities today—because they can.

In his response to Wooster's petition, Smith noted that 12 Blacks played during the first 14 seasons of the NFL— although there were no Black players for 13 years, there is "no evidence of any kind of boycott per se." In 1946, two Blacks (including Motley) would play in the NFL, and two more joined the Cleveland Browns of the All-American Football Conference. They were the first of thousands who would play in the modern era.

We as a nation tend to have selective historical memory when it comes to Black history, which has been recorded largely by non-Blacks and through the lens of the oppressor. Now is the time to remove the pen from the oppressors' grasp and rewrite our history through our lens to ensure that future generations are not blindfolded as we were.

Using never-before-heard stories passed down and shared by Charles Follis' family members, this book seeks to correct part of Black history. Only through his family one can really understand who Charles Follis was and what he was able to accomplish. He endured unimaginable racist atrocities and personal tragedy— including the deaths of two brothers—just to play football.

Because he did, football was able to prosper.

CHAPTER 1

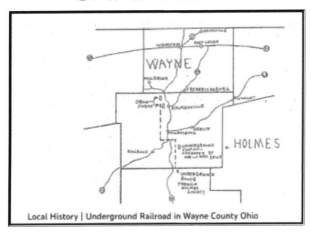

Local History | Underground Railroad in Wayne County Ohio

Up from Slavery

Confronting the blistering wind of a northern Virginia winter, James "Henry" Follis hurriedly gathers firewood to heat a small farmhouse at the feet of the Blue Ridge Mountains.

Each time Henry returns with a load, a little warmth leaks from the humble home. He checks his two daughters, Lelia and Cora Belle, wrapping them tightly in blankets, then tends to his wife, Catherine, who is struggling to deliver their third child in four years.

The familiarity makes it no less painful. There is resistance against every push; the baby is in an awkward, twisted position. Henry worries the umbilical cord might be wrapped around the baby's neck when he notices that this child is coming feet first. The young parents work together, and Catherine gives birth to a baby boy, his fight for life only just beginning.

A freed slave, Henry dares to imagine the far reaches of "freedom," but in Botetourt County, Virginia, the obstacles still seem endless. Still, Catherine and Henry, who married in 1875, grew up as slaves. They're willing to risk it all so that their children experience everything "freedom" has to offer. The Follis family has always clung to their hope and their faith in God. It has fueled them in times of crisis, and Henry has always managed to navigate them through troubled waters.

Years before the Thirteenth Amendment abolished slavery (at least, officially on paper), Henry's father, Benjamin Follis, had his heart and mind set on freedom. Born in 1820, Benjamin was a slave who was observant and resourceful. He remembers Nat Turner's Rebellion in 1831 as a child and it inspired him to dream of life outside of his current conditions. Aware of the influence from the north with such heroism as John Browns failed raid attempt on Harpers Ferry in 1859 to free the slaves; Benjamin plans for his move North. In 1878, he packs up his family and leaves Cloverdale shortly before the growing season. Knowing the hearts of former slaveholders would never be emancipated from hatred,

Benjamin decides to take advantage of his new power to leave Virginia. He settles his family in Wooster, Ohio—a cultured town with a growing textile industry and fertile farmland.

Benjamin's lot becomes only the second Black family to settle in Wooster—ironically, his first residence was in an old Underground Railroad safe house. Though religiously diverse, Wooster is a tight-knit community that was well known to run-away slaves seeking freedom in the north. Several homes were frequently utilized by slaves as "safe-houses":

> **Watters House** - home located at 714 Pittsburgh Ave. was built before 1860. Reportedly was a stop on the underground railroad before the Civil War. At a much later date it once operated as a dance hall.
>
> **Fifer House** - large square wood frame house located at 1575 Burbank Rd. was built before 1873. Reportedly was a stop on the underground railroad before the Civil War and has a double-roof in the attic where people could be hidden while staying in the house.
>
> **Jeffries House** - brick house with steep roof lines and fancy exterior trim located at 745 Pittsburgh Ave. was built about 1845. A stop for run-away slaves.

Ultimately, they build their own homes on Spink Street.

Benjamin has no intention of working in the fields again. He plans to make the most of this move. He's good with numbers, good with money—that makes him a rare commodity. Blacks are still widely prohibited from learning, reading and arithmetic in 1878, even in the more-progressive Ohio. Benjamin asks for a job at the local bank, and—in the first of many firsts to come for the Follis family—Benjamin becomes the first Black man to work in the Wooster Firestone Bank.

Realizing early on that the opportunities in Wooster far outweighed those in Virginia, Benjamin encourages Henry to follow him and move his family north. He knows the challenges Henry faces daily, and he also longs for the family to be reunified. Henry would have done exactly that, but he and Catherine are committed to establishing a family and creating his own business in Virginia.

They are also intrigued by Ohio, as their white neighbors in Cloverdale and Buchanan—angry about The Emancipation and are sympathetic to the Lost Cause— have twice tried to torch their home. But Henry remains defiant. The scars of slavery remind him that this life, though imperfect, is better.

He works as a coachman—a toilsome job that takes him away for long stretches and barely feeds his family. Each day, the angry stares of white passengers try to put him in his place. He has been stashing away every extra nickel and dime to forge a path in the Buchanan-

Cloverdale corridor, once a Confederate stronghold.

Finally, as the sun rises, Catherine can breathe easy. In her arms rests her newborn son: Charles Walter Follis. As she and Henry admire their son, they probably wonder how he will fare in this violent white world.

Henry now has a new obstacle: feeding *three* children. Few skilled jobs exist for freed slaves. He was just 12 years old when the Civil War began to ravage everything from Manassas to Petersburg to Richmond. Like blood into the battlefields, hate and resentment soaked into slaves as the war raged on—but unlike that blood, those feelings remained long after the "Slaveowner's Rebellion" concluded. There is no escaping being Black.

Henry needs more income than his coachman's job provides. He could try the mill in Buchanan, or the train station in Roanoke, but as former slave owners are tightening their belts, Henry thinks of making his own money. He wants to lead his family to an even better life. After years of being another man's property, though, he has trouble realizing his vision. This new freedom seems to conspire against him: Blacks in Virginia still lack the right to education, even the right to worship.

Henry and Catherine decide to try cultivating their own tobacco fields. After spending years planting and harvesting crops for their slaveowners, tobacco seems easy enough; at least they could turn their 12-hour days into something for themselves. Henry sets his mind to becoming the first Black man to own and cultivate tobacco since a Colony of Virginia court recognized Angolan Anthony Johnson as a tobacco plantation owner in the 17th century. (Ultimately, Johnson's family would lose his plantation and land after his death.) However, the work is grueling, and Henry hasn't even money enough for a free smoke. Soon, he'll have his son to join him in the fields, but holding out that long must seem impossible. He is stubborn, but not impractical. He knows being an independent tobacco farmer comes with the inevitable risks of having his fields burned or destroyed. Black families all over the Deep South—particularly in South Carolina—would see their land and property usurped by courts and big textile companies following Reconstruction and begin moving North and West in significant numbers. Those numbers grow in the 1890s as Black land ownership and wealth diminish even further. Rather than concede to white resistance, Henry shrewdly manipulates distrust into unlikely partnerships —keeping in mind those white businessmen can pull the plug the moment he agrees to surrender large shares of his profits to pay for seed advanced for the following spring.

On a cool summer night in 1881, Henry and Catherine watch Charles circle the house in a frenzy. At two years old, he's already overflowing with energy. Of course, the boy has no idea that his family's fate depends on the "generosity" of tobacco plantation owners, nor that his father is on the verge of losing everything.

Instead of cash, Henry is often compensated with IOUs and unwanted goods. One "here you go" is a ragged baseball glove. Henry is insulted but keeps it. Charles digs it out of storage, then treasures it.

Like many Blacks, Charles has never seen a baseball game, but it doesn't keep him from dreaming. Fascinated by his father's stories of Fleetwood Walker, Home Run Johnson, and Frank Grant, Charles has become enthralled by baseball. Sadly, even at five, Charles is hardly naïve. He also knows Black baseball players can't play professionally with white players. He has heard Henry discussing baseball with fellow sharecroppers and absorbs their incisive commentary about Blacks being excluded from a sport they play better than the whites getting paid for it. (Henry, for his part, can't help thinking the same thing is true for Black tobacco farmers.) In the Northeast and Midwest, things seemed somewhat different: Negro baseball teams are thriving in places like Brooklyn, Philadelphia, St. Louis, and Kansas City. Despite segregation, teams like the St. Louis Black Stockings and the New York-based Cuban Giants are gaining popularity in the 1880s. Already, perhaps, Henry is dreaming of his son circling bases one day so that he never has to work a day in a field.

First in Major League Baseball - Moses Fleetwood Walker 1884

While baseball is appealing, Henry and Catherine have other ambitions for their children. They speak of the Tuskegee Institute, a new college founded by fellow Virginia native Booker T. Washington. Henry has earned some measure of success and respect largely because he has learned to read and write—tools whites either admired or feared. However, he's also aware that the Ku Klux Klan has launched an active campaign to keep Blacks from attaining intellectual gains. The Klan began months after the defeat of the Confederate army and end of the Civil War in 1866, as defeated angry whites were determined to restore their right to enslave blacks and restore white supremacy by any means necessary. In a series of devastating decisions, the United States Supreme Court blocked Congressional efforts to protect formerly enslaved people. In decision after decision, the Court ceded control to the same white Southerners who used terror and violence to stop Black political participation, upheld laws and practices codifying racial hierarchy, and embraced a new constitutional order defined by "states' rights."

Within a decade after the Civil War, Congress began to abandon the promise of assistance to millions of formerly enslaved Black people. Violence, mass lynchings, and lawlessness enabled white Southerners to create a regime of white supremacy and Black disenfranchisement alongside a new economic order that continued to exploit Black labor. White officials in the North and West similarly rejected racial equality, codified racial discrimination, and occasionally embraced the same tactics of violent racial control seen in the South.

The Equal Justice Initiative has indicated more than 2,000 Black victims were killed during the Reconstruction era, from 1865 to 1876. This compared to the more than 4,400 killings documented for the 74-year era of racial terror lynching from 1877 to 1950. — *Equal Justice Initiative, "Reconstruction in America: Racial Violence after the Civil War, 1865-1876" (2020).*

The Klans terror continues to this day.

Henry and Catherine are still haunted by the memories of their home being set ablaze by white men in the spring of 1881. His daughters and Charles are old enough to remember the flames engulfing their home, but it feels like a lifetime ago. The episode anneals Henry, preparing him to stare unblinkingly into the dark, menacing eyes of racism.

Henry holds onto his coachman's job, and his Black neighbors pitch in when it's time to plant and harvest. Even with white plantation owners demanding the lion's share of any profits, he manages to squirrel away a little money. Over an 18-month span, Charles gets three more siblings—sister Laura Alice, and twin brothers Allen and James (affectionately known as "Jimmy"). Henry's three-child concern has ballooned to a six-child concern; he starts to wonder how much better life might be outside of Botetourt County.

The decision to leave is difficult. After all, it's the only home of their own that they've ever known, and Catherine has a seventh child, Curtis Washington Follis, on the way. Yet, run-ins with disgruntled plantation owners are growing more heated, and their young children don't yet understand the full dangers of being Black.

In the winter of 1884, Catherine pleads with Henry after being up for three straight nights fighting off members of the KKK to get some much-needed rest.

When Henry let his guard down, just for a night... the house bellowed an eerie sound that's a parent's worst nightmare... one of the girls was screaming uncontrollably... this awoken Henry who immediately understood what had occurred. His home, the one he built as a freed slave was again engulfed in flames.

The kids screaming uncontrollably, Henry scurries about from one corner of the burning home trying to shepherd their children safely outside.

In the panic and furious pace, he does not account for little Allen who was always a curious energetic boy. Henry then with a local neighbor begins to attempt another entry but as the fire begins to engulf his home he makes the decision that no man must make. He stares at the black soot faces of Catherine, Lelia, Cora, Laura, Charles, Jimmy and Curtis and knows he will not return if he enters and at that moment the home of Henry and Catherine Follis collapses along with their dreams and the life of their twin son Allen.

The look on the face of his father will be forever etched in Charles' memory.

The tragic death of three-year-old Allen is agonizing for Henry and Catherine, who are too numb to feel the pain of a fire that has left the family homeless. The elder children each separately take a certain blame for the loss of Allen and are having a terrible time coping with his sudden disappearance from the sibling pact. In the days to come for Jimmy, his repeated calls for "Al" haunt the Follis family and for the first time in their lives, hopelessness prevails. Whatever life they have in Cloverdale has reached its breaking point. In 1884, tired of sleeping one eye open and a rifle within reach, Henry and Catherine decide it's time. They can no longer spend any more of their lives in a state that devalues, demeans, and dismisses them because they're Black.

Even as a freed slave, it won't be easy to walk away from Cloverdale. The white plantation owners who have reaped the benefits of Henry's sweat equity are furious. They see his desires for a better life as disloyalty and can't believe he would leave them to cultivate and harvest their own tobacco fields.

Nonetheless, in mid-December, for the sake of his family, Henry leaves his family with a trusted neighbor and makes the solo trip to Wooster Ohio in 1884 for which he purchased a lot. He then makes the trip back to Virginia to retrieve his family securing a shift on a train bound for Ohio.

> Wayne County Recorder Property Transfers
> • 1884: Simon Bender, Lydia Bender To James H. Follis Vol. 111 p.547 Lot 804 $450

Reportedly, Ohio is a land of promising opportunities. Its serpentine rivers might offer Henry a chance to cultivate his own land. There is hope they can thrive in a more progressive part of the country where being Black would still be hard, but far less treacherous.

That point speaks to Henry, who has seen enough hard and treacherous. He's been working since his spindly legs could hold him up. Catherine is a year older than her husband, and years wiser; after all, she's given birth to seven children. Born into slavery, Catherine has never left Virginia. Whatever lies ahead must be better for her young daughters than her past. She is comforted knowing, at the very least, that they'll never have to see their siblings snatched away by the slave trade.

They're not timid about the move, though; Henry does know of one Black family already living and working in Wooster, Ohio. The thought of reuniting with his father comforts Henry as the train marches through the night.

CHAPTER 2

Journey to Destiny

◆ ◆ ◆

The long ride along ragged rails from the foothills of Virginia has the entire Follis family feeling anxious about their journey's end. They make it through the mountainous trails of West Virginia and the winding, narrow tracks of the Ohio River Valley without a hitch. Every now and then, Henry reminds himself that life on Tobacco Road has become a place where even strong, somewhat financially secure Black families struggle to survive.

Henry has little idea what to expect other than Ohio must offer something better than Botetourt County. He and Catherine are aware that Ohio is a refuge for acclaimed abolitionists such as John Brown, Sojourner Truth, and Harriet Tubman. Even though Ohio outlawed slavery back in 1802 (a year before it was granted statehood), like other northern territories, Ohio's laws still allow for fugitive slaves—and sometimes freed slaves —to be reclaimed by their owners. Bounties of $1,000

($33,000 today) were awarded to anyone that reports a runaway slave, leading to a capture became a very lucrative incentive for some.

Many freed slaves had migrated from the misery of plantation work, causing a reduction in the workforce for plantation owners often eager to return freed slaves to some form of shackles. Henry and Catherine have no sympathy for their former slaveowners. They've endured far greater pains: loss of freedom, loss of home, loss of property, loss of family, and loss of humanity. Hope is at a premium, yet they persevere with the hope that someday they will find a place where their children could grow up unhindered by the color of their skin.

Henry begins to wonder if he's made the right decision. Will his family have to glance over their shoulders as they did in Cloverdale? Catherine squeezes his massive hand, and Henry pledges better days ahead.

The train powers along the nearby Tuscarawas River; it veers northeast toward Stark and Wayne Counties as the sun sets. There are no mountains on the horizon. Rather, the landscape is dominated by cornfields. Most noticeably, there are no tobacco plantations.

Before heading north to Cleveland, the train stops in Canton, Ohio to pick up some more passengers. Henry likes what he sees, and he surprises his family when he decides it's time to look around: He has heard of Negro families making their way to nearby Akron or Ravenna. Catherine had a soft inquiry about Akron, due to Sojourner Truth's 1851 speech there, commonly titled "Ain't I a Woman," was an encouragement for the aspiring to be free slaves of the South.

Things seem okay, but Henry doesn't really know what to expect from the local white folks. They aren't quite Yankees, yet they are slightly more civil than the Southern whites he and his brother Coleman encountered working the railroads down in South Carolina and Georgia. Yet, as the Follises reconvene on the platform, no one addresses them as if they do not belong. Already, Canton feels nothing like Cloverdale or Buchanan. Still, white men, still coming to grips with the abolishment of slavery, could be wildly unpredictable.

As Catherine and Henry are busy gathering the family's belongings, five-year-old Charles wanders into the train station. He sees a newspaper outside a shop and becomes transfixed by illustrations depicting a baseball game. The clerk notices the Black boy fingering his wares and demands he put the newspaper back. When Charles asks if he can have the paper, he is told to leave. When Charles refuses, the storekeeper again points him toward the door. This time, Charles relents and puts the newspaper down.

As he turns to walk away, Charles spots something even more fascinating: a catcher's mitt. He wants to get it for his brothers; the one his father gave him is packed safely away.

Before Charles can even ask how much the glove costs, the clerk barks: "Get out of here before I throw you out!"

Charles is shaken to his core. He wants to counter with a verbal jab, but even at his age, he knows he's in dangerous waters. Suddenly, he feels alone and frightened. Then, he overcomes his fears, and asks: "How much?"

The clerk looks at Charles as if he's lost his mind. *The nerve of this little Black kid.* Of course, Charles' tenacity was learned behavior: He has watched his father stubbornly negotiate and out-fox plantation owners all throughout the Roanoke corridor.

"Get out!" the storekeeper hollers. "I'm not giving you that glove. Now, get!"

Henry fails to notice that Charles has wandered off. No matter how many times he tells the children to stay put, one of them was bound to drift aimlessly.

Suddenly, Charles lumbers out of the train station looking as if someone snatched out his heart. Henry knows something has happened inside the station but worries about ruffling white folks feathers.

Catherine's fear for her son overwhelms her with anger. She remembers the last time she saw that expression:

Months earlier, Henry and Charles are in a general store in Buchanan when the storekeeper accuses a 12-year-old Black boy of stealing molasses. They hear the storekeeper shout: "You little nigger! That'll be the last time you put your nigger hands on anything."

Later during that same evening, that 12-year-old boy was swinging from a tree.

There is no such thing as a veiled threat. Yesterday, molasses. Today, a baseball glove. Tomorrow? The angry, piercing words of the clerk probably feel like a verbal noose tightening around Charles' young neck. How could he not hear the worst in them: *You little nigger! If you touch that glove one more time, it will be the last breath you breathe!*

Charles' young life has been shaped by any number of atrocities, but the image of that young boy being lynched for allegedly stealing something worth about a dime is tattooed on his mind. For such a young child, the incident and others witnessed by him leads to the rapid erosion of childlike trust and the realization that his world will be nothing but hostile.

Catherine holds him tight, hoping to guard him from the inevitable pains that lie ahead for a young Black boy in America. Henry can't find the right words to console his dejected son. Though he wants to let the slight pass, Catherine is livid. She storms into the station, finds the clerk, and asks him pointedly: "What did you do to my son?"

All the white folks in the station stop dead in their tracks.

"He wants that," the clerk snaps back, pointing at the secondhand catcher's mitt atop a small stack of other worn baseball gloves. "What *you* gonna do with a baseball glove?"

Catherine doesn't know the answer; all she knows is that Charles and Lelia usually fool around outside, playing catch with something resembling a ball. She cares little for baseball herself, but she recalls that her slaveowner's children loved to play baseball on the dirt roads of Cloverdale.

FOLLIS: GREATNESS TRANSCENDS

"What do you want for it?" Catherine asks.

The clerk doesn't answer. Rather, he looks away and asks, "What's *your* boy gonna do with it?"

Before Catherine can snap back, Henry marches into the station. He approaches the clerk and offers, as barter, a pocketful of change and a few loose cigarettes. He stands there with his hand extended, waiting for the clerk to accept his silent offer. The white customers stare at this tall Negro man whose granite jaw complements his cold stare. The clerk rolls his eyes and accepts. Everyone watches silently as Henry exits the station with the mitt in one hand and his wife's hand in the other.

Charles' eyes gleam with joy as Henry gives him the glove. He says nothing, just wraps his arms around his father. Henry smiles, then realizes it's time to board the train and get the hell out of Canton before the clerk changes his mind. As the train's engines roar again, Catherine counts heads: Lelia, Cora, Laura, Curtis, and Jimmy are all accounted for. She gasps a bit before finding Charles cuddling up next to Henry, gently caressing his glove.

Henry grows increasingly nervous as the train nears their destination. Wooster is rooted in the heart of a county named after Mad Anthony Wayne, a notorious Army general who twice led his troops to convincing victories over Native Americans. (Wayne, who would later go into politics, was unceremoniously booted from Congress for casting a fraudulent vote.) Long before the Follises arrive, Native Americans of the Wooster region are forced to surrender this land and their ways of life. From the Annals of Wayne County History:

> The natives of Ashango-land are fortified and grow garrulous over the charm-working and superstitious myths of their Black progenitors, and the savage Indian has his repertory of hoarded legendary story, and is as familiar with the traditionary annals of his ancient tribes ... It can be maintained, then, not as a fact or an abstraction, but as a principle entrenched in a sound and practical philosophy that nothing can more interest a people or a community than a history of the times in which they have lived—a reproduction of the drama in which their fathers were the actors.

Knowing this much, Henry is determined to make this land his home—hoping it will be a place where his children will have a chance to fulfill the lofty dreams he had while working his fingers to the bone in Virginia. But he also knows the Follises and other Black families will need to work even harder to avoid the same fate in Wooster.

For some Black families, Ohio is a temporary stay until they can figure out a way to move their families farther west—to Chicago or Detroit or Kansas City—where the prospects of work are reportedly better.

As the boys are taking turns pounding Charles' scuffed-up glove into shape, Catherine holding Curtis, with little Laura closely in tow, makes her way to a window to observe the largely untamed land of Wayne County. For the first time since they left Virginia, Henry can exhale. Soon, he'll be reunited with his father, Benjamin, who has worked tirelessly to ready everything for his son's arrival.

Finally, the train rolls into the station at Depot Street in Orrville—a sleepy, quaint town 10 miles southwest of Wooster. There's no need to stretch their legs, so the Follises stay aboard until the conductor steers the Pennsylvania Railroad toward their final stop. When a curious Charles ventures near the exit door, Henry keeps him within arm's reach. Beyond Orville, the train winds through a smattering of small farm towns with rows of corn separated by endless rows of corn. They can smell the livestock sprawled about acres of grassland perfect for a family of eight.

There is nothing wrong with dreaming. After all, dreams have gotten them this far.

Henry's family arrives at a time when there are plenty of jobs for laborers and sharecroppers. It'll be a few days before he and Catherine can settle into their new home at 818 Spink Street, where Black families have been "encouraged" to congregate. Henry settles his family a stone's throw away from Benjamin's stead.

The haunting memories of arson and lynching still linger for Catherine, so she focuses on making sure her daughters will receive the education she was never afforded. However, of the 5,800 inhabitants of Wooster in 1888, fewer than 20 are Black. Until they can be admitted to the First Ward—a school on Wooster's east side—Catherine decides to home-school the children. The Follis kids are still somewhat edgy. They are different from other kids in this middle-of-nowhere town.

In fact, they are no longer kids at all.

CHAPTER 3

Rising above the Noise

❖ ❖ ❖

Albeit slowly, Wooster's Black population grows in the five years that follow. A few more Black families have come, settling mostly on the city's west side. The numbers are still too small yet to call the enclave a "Black community," but it has become a safe area where they can assimilate without feeling totally isolated.

The Follis men make a pact to live by the fundamental principle of meritocracy. Wooster is a small town with religious foundations and liberal thinking—just the place for men who feel at their core that they are limited only by their own imaginations and abilities to achieve their aspirations. "Let Us Have Men," an article by John Harman appearing in the 1893 *Wooster High School Annual*, encapsulates the prevailing thinking of the community and its young men: "What we need is men; not nobles, princes, kings; but noble, princely, kingly men—men in every sense the word implies. We need men in whom we can place entire confidence."

The Follis men arrive at the perfect time to fill that void, and that confluence allows the family to continue to blossom. To the family, this signals that God's hand has led them exactly where they need to be. As is their habit, they lead the charge to instill a sense of independence among Black families, especially those still having trouble adjusting to freedom. Some are uncomfortable beyond the boundaries of their plantations; others are still chained to the mental shackles of slavery. Having endured the loss of not only their home but also their child, they have left those shackles in Virginia. Henry has kept his family's destiny afloat by standing firm against the white men who committed those crimes. Still, no matter how much influence they build among Wooster's Black population, the Follises grapple with the undeniable reality that danger could be around any corner.

Benjamin has established himself as a smart, capable businessman. Well before his son arrives, he discovers that the road to social and financial freedom is littered with obstacles—chief among them an inadequate and biased judicial system that swallows up young black men without due process. In that respect, he finds Ohio is more similar to Virginia than he hoped.

Benjamin parlays his job at the bank into opportunities for his Black neighbors so he can help develop a system that ensures young Black men have a chance at equality and the possibility of surviving minor criminal mistakes.

Though the family is doing everything to avoid these dangers, they cannot avoid the realities of their shade, and they are unable to escape the cruel injustices of 1886.

The boys generally keep to themselves in order to avoid the inescapable trouble seeking out young Black men. They do not have to be told to stay away from white girls and women. They know even a misinterpreted look could be fatal. Jimmy is the most curious of Catherine's sons. Like many six-year-olds, Jimmy gets caught with his hand in the cookie jar more than once, so it's Charles' job to make sure his little brother stays in line—a mighty responsibility for a boy just two years older and also recovering from the loss of his brother, Allen (Jimmy's twin). They have become inseparable already; wherever Charles goes, Jimmy is right by his side.

Trouble, though, has a way of finding Black boys like Jimmy.

In February 1886, another seemingly routine trip to a local will unravel the fabric of the Follis household and put Jimmy's parents into a precarious position.

Like most young children, Jimmy is fascinated by shiny objects. When an absent-minded customer leaves several pieces of jewelry on the store counter, Jimmy looks but doesn't touch. As Catherine and her sons are leaving the store, the customer—a white woman—notices her brooch is missing. Predictably, she disregards the slew of other white customers and fingers Jimmy for the theft. Before Catherine and the boys can walk half a block, the outraged woman chases them down and demands the return of her ten-dollar brooch.

"My boy wouldn't steal a thing." Catherine tells her. "Everyone knows it; *you* know it."

The woman persists, hailing a Wooster policeman, who ignores Catherine's pleas of innocence. Charles watches as the policeman corners his mother on the street and lectures her about Jimmy's behavior, then looks on in disbelief as his little brother is interrogated and searched. There's nothing in his pockets, nothing up his sleeve, no jewelry anywhere.

"You know my son didn't do this," Catherine says again. "You know who we are. You know our family—and you know *Jimmy*."

But none of that matters to the patrolman. A white woman has accused a Black boy of stealing. Catherine, who has become one of the most respected women in Wooster—Black or white—is dismissed as a liar covering up for a thieving son. For her, the question isn't about guilt or innocence: It's about saving her son from an all-too-familiar charge of "shopping while Black."

She's too angry to cry. Again, she pleads, "You know he

didn't do this."

Though no evidence exists, Jimmy—just six years old —is charged with theft.

Henry, who has promised his family better times, now has to find his son a way out of trouble. For if he fails, what will become of Jimmy? Would Curtis, Charles, Laura, Cora, or Lelia be next? What if some overzealous white woman wanted to ruin their lives as well? Just how close was Charles to suffering the same fate in Canton? And what of Charles now? He surely feels this is all his fault ... Even with his spotless reputation in Wooster, Henry finds himself between a rock and a hard place. He has to achieve the best possible outcome for his son in a system skewed to his disadvantage. In a pained whisper, he tells a crying Catherine: "There's nothing we can do; we just gotta keep fighting."

Catherine rebels with anger. Win or lose, she's ready to wage war. Suddenly, she wonders why the Follises engage in so many battles they are willing to concede. She is unwilling to allow the legal system to undo the fabric of her family as it had so many others, stitch by stitch. What if ripping Jimmy from their arms is only the beginning? She can't bring herself to picture him in that dreary, crowded courthouse jail—yet one more name on the never-ending list of imprisoned Black men. Nothing could be worse than losing Allen, she thinks; then she considers losing both.

Jimmy is tossed behind bars with far older peers already hardened by routine harassment and vicious beatings. But the real danger comes from the police, who threaten to beat a confession out of Jimmy. They're convinced he's stolen the brooch, but he has broken a bigger law: arousing the suspicion of a white woman. The jailers soon reckon they can coerce the other inmates to do their dirty work, but too many know the Follises. Their collective defiance incenses the officers, who yank Jimmy from the cell to administer a frighteningly familiar brand of justice.

Immediately, Jimmy's survival instincts kick in. As police drag him across the holding-cell floor, Jimmy does not protest. When they slam him against the wall, he does not strike back. When they badger him to confess, he does not concede. They batter him, but he remains defiant. The policemen, incensed by the six-year-old, double their efforts.

After two hours of verbal and physical abuse, Jimmy is returned to his cell. His beaten body collapses against the cold brick wall. A long night grows even longer—his bruises too fresh to move, his fear too great to sleep. Why, he must have wondered, why his parents did not save him from all this unnecessary pain?

Catherine and Henry are unsure of Jimmy's fate as they arrive at the courthouse downtown. Catherine's spirits are lifted when Jimmy's accuser fails to appear for the hearing. It's an admission, it seems, that the police and the accuser overreached. Surely, the mayor would, at the maximum, slap Jimmy on the wrist for being in the wrong place at the wrong time while being Black.

Catherine renders one final plea before the mayor delivers his verdict: "I know my son, and he's not who she says he is!" she cries, this time uncontrollably, as if she knows what's coming.

Henry sits silently, his hands pressing on his knees. His eyes scan the courtroom as if he's searching for the right words. He can feel Catherine staring at him, waiting for him to offer some defense—something to sway the court toward leniency. He finds nothing but deafening silence.

Suddenly, Henry is overcome with a foreign sensation: an angered panic when he sees Jimmy's appearance. Henry inexplicably decides that changing Jimmy's plea to guilty will evoke the very leniency Catherine is seeking. He reverses the earlier not-guilty plea he entered for his son to guilty. After speaking out of turn, Henry contritely tells the judge: "We promise you won't see him here again. He's a good boy."

The outburst backfires. The mayor not only demands a fine, but he also dispassionately sentences Jimmy to the Lancaster Industrial School for Delinquents. Though they have fought to achieve some acceptance among Wooster's white elite, the Follis' son is added to the countless Black kids the courts are tossing into reform schools—slave labor by another name.

Henry, blaming himself, is gutted. The ordeal also severs the bond of trust between him and Catherine. He prays the damage is repairable, but hopelessness permeates his every thought.

Jimmy's case changes how the Follises view their white neighbors as well. All the goodwill and faith restored in whites since they have come to Ohio dissipates as Henry and Catherine are left asking God why they must endure losing *two* sons.

When it comes time for Jimmy to be admitted to reform school, Henry is coerced into signing a document misrepresenting his son's age. Though Jimmy has only recently turned seven, signed court documents state that James Henry Follis relinquishes an "eight-year-old" Jimmy to the custody of the state (the minimum age a child could be turned over to reform schools). Some Black kids in the late 19th century never returned from reform school, Jimmy being no different.

Jimmy Follis vs. State of Ohio, sent to reform school in 1886.

◆ ◆ ◆

On January 30, 1888, Catherine gives birth to the last of her five sons—Joseph Walter Wayne Follis. Two years later, on March 14, 1890, Lucile Jane Follis is born, bringing the Follis children to eight—four boys and four girls. Their parents pray they'll be able to envision their lives through anything but the marred lens of hatred and despair.

The only benefit to their hardships is that the Follises have learned to adapt to their mostly white environment. Rather than rely on white businessmen, they put their stock in faith to guide them through their challenges. Along with other local spiritual leaders, the Follises work to bring Wooster's entire Black community—now approaching 100 people—closer to faith. They establish a place of worship inside an engine house on Spink Street, just a few blocks away from the Follis home.

Surprisingly, a few of their white neighbors also invite the Follises to worship at the First Baptist Church (now Bethany Baptist Church). Henry is among four Black men who meet with First Baptist pastors and officers at the home of Reverend R. L. Morrison with the aim of establishing a Second Baptist Church. In the end, they are able to broker an agreement that Black members of Wooster's community will cherish for generations.

Second Baptist Church built by James "Henry" Follis.

In October 1892, the cornerstone of Second Baptist is laid at a cost of $2,400. Henry leads an effort to raise additional funds so that the church can hold its first service in 1894. His skills as a carpenter offset the brunt of the labor cost.

As Wooster's entire Black population starts to gain traction, particularly in business, Benjamin's work at the bank allows him to monitor the finances of several Black families while giving financial advice as needed. His job also enables him to learn how to finance the building of Second Baptist Church.

The church becomes more than a place to give praise: It's a refuge for those Blacks still finding their way and a school where mothers can bring their children and properly educate them in both mind and spirit. As a sanctuary of sanity and peace, Second Baptist also represents the Black community's unyielding faith in God. It perfectly illustrates the community's willingness to join hands and rise above the noise of racism.

The entire community—Blacks and many whites— respect the Follis family for their willingness to fight against discrimination. Henry and Catherine are steadfast in their belief; they aren't going to allow prejudice and racism to change what they believe, even if most white people viewed Blacks as ungodly. Elevating Black consciousness in a predominantly white town positions the Follises to become one of the most consequential Black families in Northeast Ohio. The people of Wooster are starting to notice Black aspirations are greater than they imagined.

Their expectations of success are a rising tide.

1940 OFFICERS AND TRUSTEES

FIRST ROW — Clora Taliaferro, W.L. Hamilton, Mrs. P.W. Woods
SECOND ROW — Samuel King, Thomas Price, P.W. Woods, Ewart L. Pringle
THIRD ROW — Edward Richardson, Joseph Follis, Harper Reynolds

Grandpa Joseph Follis (top-center)

CHAPTER 4

The Legend Begins

◆ ◆ ◆

[Charles] was a very wonderful player. He was as good a player as there was ... agile ... tremendous. If he were alive, he could play on any football team now. Charles was built for a game beyond his time. With the forward pass never an option, every defender could hone in on Charles who was tasked with churning out the five yards needed, then to move the first-down sticks. It was first-and-five instead of first-and-ten, and the offense had to get those yards in three downs instead of four, usually through the guard or tackle. —Walter Mougey, Wooster High School Class of 1902.

At 19, Charles Follis is like most Black teenagers during the latter days of the 19th century. He vaguely understands the cultural divide even in a town homogenous as Wooster. He imagines the future little; the present is more pressing.

His parents understand how important education will be for their children, but that's easier said than done for Black kids. Though Henry received no formal schooling, he knows how slave owners would ensure Blacks were incapable of thinking for themselves. Lelia, Cora, and Laura were very fortunate in that regard. In the years before Charles can enroll in school, the sisters not only teach him how to read and write but encourage him to develop his incredible singing voice.

Singing and schooling both help, but all Charles really wants to do is hit a baseball—for a professional team. As the first frost hits in 1899, he grows restless knowing he'll have an entire winter before that's possible.

Charles reminds Henry of his own father, Benjamin. Sold twice while enslaved, Benjamin has focused his restlessness to his advantage, moving from place to place until he secured both his homestead and community position in Wooster. Henry suggests that, if Charles cannot play baseball, he should focus his energies on something else. For Charles, that something else becomes football.

Though the Follis brothers have yet to attend a football game, they've heard and read about local teams like the Akron Athletic Club, Canton Bulldogs, Newark Athletic Club, and Shelby Athletic Association. Though Ohio will someday become a hotbed for football, the game has yet to capture the attention of their devoutly religious pocket of the state. There are a couple teams in town—Wooster

College and Wooster Athletic Association—but neither has developed any real fanbase.

Their mother finds the sport unnecessarily violent and barbaric, but their father is happy to throw his weight behind anything that collectively excites his sons. The problem is there's no time for play. In addition to their chores, the boys are knee-deep in all church matters —choir, ushering, and youth ministry.

Charles Follis (centered) with Wooster High School Class of 1900.

Charles becomes one of the first Black male students to attend Wooster High School, where his sister, Cora, became the first Black female student to graduate. Henry and Catherine worry Charles will be ridiculed for being older than the other students, but they also know he'll be opening the door for younger brothers Curtis and Joe.

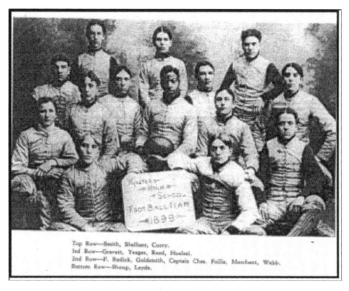

The first Wooster High School football team of 1899. Captain Charles Follis (centered).

Though he had a late start on his formal education, he was intellectually ahead and clearly more mature than his peers when classes began. Luckily, Charles is familiar with many of his classmates from church functions. Others have seen Charles sing in various revivals, and their parents and families probably remember attending Charles' rendition of "Standin' in the Need o' Prayer." No doubt Charles' age, powerful stature, and booming voice play a role, but he commands respect at Wooster High from Day One. Instead of being a target, he disarms his classmates with his charming personality.

Suddenly, Catherine is worrying less that white kids will hate her son and more that they might misunderstand his intentions. Worse yet, what if they suddenly decide he's just some highfaluting Negro who's too big for his breeches. (Kids are one thing, but their crazy fathers out in the sticks are something else entirely.) The Follis children understand their mother is bothered less by the sport's violence than by its perceived lack of purpose. Still, Charles is determined to play. He sees in football the potential to shatter society's limitations, and he sets out to establish a program at Wooster High School.

Surprisingly, Catherine changes her tune: If Charles can convince white kids that he can lead them on a football field, she's all for it. In just a few weeks, Charles has a varsity team up and running; his teammates elect him captain. Shortly thereafter, Catherine is beaming as Second Baptist Church trustee Richard Morrison declares to the congregation that Charles has successfully established the Wooster High football team. Congregants even remark such a mission could even help bridge Wooster's racial divide.

As the Black community starts its rise in Wooster, Charles—in the spotlight—becomes a standard bearer. Though the pressure must be immense, both Curtis and Joe are anxious to follow in his footsteps.

Perhaps, Catherine has to admit, football has a purpose after all.

In the days leading up to Wooster's inaugural game, the Charles Follis-led team is scurrying about the neighborhood doing odd jobs to help their parents pay for the equipment, uniforms, and shoes needed. The 14-man team had to look like they were ready to play. The rush to prepare means the team is unable to squeeze in as many practices as Alliance, their first opponent.

Some community leaders are pushing back against the high school having an organized football team. As a result, few adults are clamoring to head the team, and Charles is thrust into the position of player-coach.

For this game, his plan is simple: Give me the ball and let me steamroll to the endzone. The Wooster Republican reports: "The ball was kicked off and Follis brought it back halfway across the field, plunging through Alliance's boys as if they were so much paper."

First Football Game
October 7, 1899

Wooster High School Scoops the University Boys.

An exciting event in athletic circles was witnessed last Saturday forenoon in Wooster on the University Campus by a large assemblage of friends interested in physical as well as mental culture, which go hand in hand at popular institutions of learning. It was a foot ball contest, skillfully and warmly played by teams of Wooster High School and of University Preparatory Department, resulting in the High School winning by a score of 10 to 0.

It is reported that Prof. Haupert, Superintendent of the Wooster schools, is delighted with the outcome and vigorously "rooted" for his boys, and that the President of the University, though saying nothing at present, is Holden up for future events. The line up of the teams was as follows:

High School.		University.
Goldsmith	RE	Hubbard
Webb	RT	Murray
Shoup	RG	Wood
Hoelzel	C	Turner
Yaeger	LG	McDonald
Shellhart	LT	Allis
Marchand	LE	Merrick
Curry	QB	Abby
Gravatt	LH	Mosier
Follis	RH	Perry
Smith	FB	Rochester

Wooster, like most teams, operates out of the wedge formation. At times, it looks like rugby. From the right-halfback position, Charles uses his speed and devastating power to hammer Alliance into submission.

Curtis and Joe are watching in awe. They've always known their big brother to be fast and tough. But it's the fire in his gut and the look in his eyes that inspires them. They share the joy when he scores; they feel the pain when he's taken to the ground by a swarm of Alliance players, as one defender after another tries to render Charles motionless. Curtis upset over the blatant attacks on Charles looks as though he's ready to storm the field until Charles gives him that smile and wink as to say, "don't worry bro watch my next play".

In the early years of football, a ball carrier is considered down only after the carrier verbally concedes (shouts "Down!"). Charles claws for every inch of ground, pile-ons be damned. Predictably, many defenders use these opportunities to take cheap shots, but Charles recognizes any lack of self-confidence can trigger the racist rants and unprovoked attacks. Like his forbears, he has seen Black men hanged fighting for basic freedoms. Touchdowns are simply another act of defiance.

The entire Wooster roster feeds off Charles' gutsy play. More importantly, they adhere to his insistence they do not retaliate.

Rowland Curry and Charles Follis
Capt. 1901   Capt. 1899

Behind his spear of (white) blockers, Charles pierces the Alliance defense again and again, out-muscling tacklers to make Wooster High's game a resounding success: a 27-0 victory over a more experienced team. In the end, Charles' actual numbers are nebulous, but the impression is lasting.

Charles isn't just a man among boys—he is an actual man—and thus he begins to form today's stereotype of the "Black student-athlete." In effect, he changes football: Game plans for both teams are now designed with Charles Follis in mind.

With Charles running behind a solid offensive line, Wooster dominates their opponents. The Wooster High defense is equally effective. Playing mostly in the middle, Charles uses his quickness and speed to thwart opposing offenses. Intracity rivals Wooster City Athletic Club and Wooster College—who recruit from the same player pool —prove to be fiercer competition, but Wooster High is able to finish 8-0, surrendering zero points all season.

If nothing else, the high school football team seems to earn the respect of lukewarm supporters. Charles and his teammates believe they're building momentum for the program. However, the community has difficulty making football a priority. In a 1975 interview in *Beacon Magazine* (formerly the *Akron Beacon Journal*), Walter D. Nice (Wooster Class of 1902), recollects how the team's second season came about. With local businesses shunning the sport, the football team launches a fundraising campaign to advance the nascent program in 1900:

> "There was a collection started to buy a football which would last the whole year. School authorities didn't give us much support. Each member of the team bought his own football, used old shoes and had cleats put on by some

shoemaker. We did our practicing just outside and north of the old school building in the park. We had just enough men to run through signals, never knowing what scrimmage was except when we played a game."

"We never had more than 14 or 15 on the squad, and we were always short of subs. For that reason, you weren't supposed to get hurt. We used as a dressing room the old furnace room, sitting around the furnace as we dressed. As for showers, we never heard of them. You would take your bath when you got home."

"The boys in those days seemed to have a football instinct and played as if their lives depended on winning the game. Football back in the early days was somewhat harder and rougher than today."

Despite all those challenges, Charles proves he's too good for high school football.

Though bigger clubs like Canton and Shelby come calling. They keep hearing about a young man known as "Follis the Speedy" exploding from Wooster's flying wedge.

Upon completing high school, Charles joins Wooster Athletic Club as an amateur. In their 1901 opener, Wooster will face Shelby Athletic Association, the defending champions of Northern Ohio. Without the same talent on his line, Charles finds himself bottled up, and Wooster fails to manufacture first downs. The 5-0 loss is Wooster's first in three years. (In the early years of professional football, touchdowns are worth five points, not six.) After their following matchup against Sebring, in which Charles registers a 100-yard touchdown run in a 28-0 victory, Wooster AC readies for their Shelby rematch. More than 2,000 fans are in attendance when Shelby rolls into town on Thanksgiving Day for the Northern Ohio Championship.

Shelby is loaded with talent, and they sometimes get help from moonlighters and mercenaries. Once such hired hand is a not-yet-famous young man named Branch Rickey, a highly intelligent halfback who's helped Shelby win a couple of titles. Charles has heard of Rickey. As Wooster College's star catcher, Charles knows that Ohio Wesleyan University has a highly touted backstop by that name.

Though a hard-fought contest, Shelby overwhelms Wooster 28-5, with Charles scoring the home side's only touchdown. Despite the disappointing loss, the Wooster Republican reports that "Follis did some splendid tackling, and his all-around playing was a feature." Charles knows the spotlight is on him, and others notice, too. Shelby's future manager, Frank C. Schiffer, already has desires on acquiring the otherworldly halfback, emphasizing he wants "Charles Follis playing with his team; not against them."

Though barnstorming with the Wooster Giants baseball team has given him a tour of Ohio, Charles has never had to pack up and live in another city. Shelby is a few hours' commute from Wooster on the "electric line," an electricity-powered streetcar connecting the rural areas of central Ohio to Cleveland. Though his parents worry what the move will mean, they understand the new independence will help Charles establish himself as his own man.

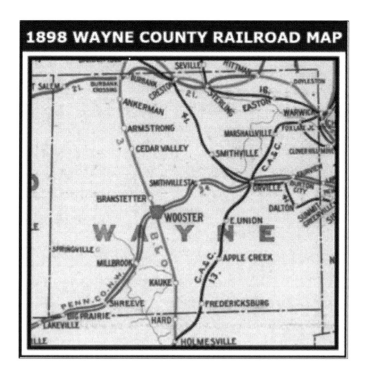

CHAPTER 5

Brothers United

◆ ◆ ◆

THE FOLLIS BROTHERS
Charles, 1900   Curt, 1903   Joe, 1904

By the late 1800s, Negroes began to disappear from professional baseball teams and were soon gone from them altogether. Now, there was never any written rule that prohibited Negroes from playing professional baseball, but soon after 1887, somehow Negroes all over couldn't get on a professional baseball team. Come to find out that all the white owners had gotten together in secret and decided to do away with Negroes in baseball. They agreed not to

add any more to their teams and to let go of the ones
they had. Called it a "gentlemen's agreement." And
I'll tell you this, the white pro-ball-club owners held
to that agreement for almost sixty years. —"Smokey"
Joe Williams in We are the Ship, The Story of Negro
League Baseball

The Follis brothers are coincidentally both far ahead
and slightly behind their time. They come of age just as
the first Negro baseball leagues are losing momentum. No
one who has witnessed the Follis brothers play the game
can deny the inevitability of professional baseball careers
in their future. They are gifted with the glove, swift on
the base paths, possess strong throwing arms, and hit
with both power and control. They possess a troika that
will someday dominate baseball: style, look, face.

"The Fabulous Follis Boys," as some Wooster residents
call them, love America's game. It's just that America's
game doesn't seem to love them back. In baseball,
perhaps more than any other professional sport of this
time, Black men are considered a threat. During the
1890s, most professional Black players are limited to
playing in exhibition games on "colored" teams on the
barnstorming circuit along with white players. In rare
instances, Black teams and white teams play each other,
and some Blacks play for all-Black teams in otherwise all-
white leagues. Of course, readers of Black publications
like the Baltimore Afro American, Pittsburgh Courier,
Kansas City Call, and Chicago Defender know Negro
leaguers are putting up big numbers. The only top white
ballplayers they face appear randomly on the circuit,

where future Hall of Famers John McGraw, Nap Lajoie, and Jimmy Collins sometimes test their mettle against the best Black players, who remarkably manage to lure white fans to their games—and steal a piece of the big-league market.

Charles' future seems to be tied to football, but his heart has never left the diamond. He not only leads the Wooster College team, he has also spent the past two years as a catcher for the Wooster Athletic Association, which captures an Ohio Trolley League title as the Wooster Giants. Charles is the team's star slugger and the league's most popular player. No one, it seems, notices the significance of a Black ballplayer integrating a college baseball team. Though his early exploits draw attention from big-league scouts, race alone keeps him from playing Major League Baseball.

Baseball soon becomes a family affair. Curtis and Joe seem born to play the game, too. In the spring of 1899, the two, despite their age difference, are inseparable—as Charles and Curtis once were. There is every expectation that Curtis will be as good as Charles—or at least his equal—when he reaches his peak. As the second son, he's stuck in the middle—five years younger than Charles, four years older than Joe. The one talent they have in common is baseball, which affords the rare opportunity to compete together. Charles and Curtis are easily the best brother tandem in Ohio. On some level, 11-year-old Joe is growing up even quicker. He's already fast—maybe even faster than Curtis—and he can handle a bat.

Some folks are called to sing, others to spread the gospel. The Follis brothers have baseball flowing through their veins. They are artists of the diamond, painting an eloquent picture of perfection—all the while singing and spreading the gospel at Second Baptist Church.

Catherine is in a much better place watching her sons play baseball. She accepts it as a rite of passage for them all, and she can't help but smile each time she sees them run the bases or make sparkling defensive plays. Now, this game has purpose—it holds the Follis boys together.

The Follis brothers are always busy working, going to school, playing football and baseball, and singing in the church. They are perhaps the most visible family in Wooster. Ultimately, that visibility creates a kind of responsibility they are prepared to accept.

In the recesses of his mind, Charles can hear his mother saying, "Don't let being Black hold you back." It's a familiar refrain in the Follis home. Catherine doesn't want any of her seven children to let doubt inhibit their expectations. She demands they do as their father has before them. Henry achieved some measure of success back in Cloverdale because he refused to minimize his expectations. Mostly, he wasn't afraid of being a Black man.

Nonetheless, Henry and his sons come to grips with a gut-wrenching truth: Major League Baseball owners and players can't stomach the idea of sharing the diamond with the sons of former slaves. It's not about winning and losing—it's about race, plain and simple.

In 1898, Curtis has grown into a rock-solid teenager with raw but promising talents in both football and baseball. He is no match yet for Charles, but he's quickly narrowing the competitive gap. Although five years separate them, Henry insists his two sons suit up for the same team in Cleveland to play against other Black players. Funnily enough, the Cleveland Spiders—a white-only team that played in the American Association and National League team from 1887 to 1899—reject every offer to face the city's all-Black or Negro league squads.

Charles and Curtis hone their skills against top-notch competition in Cleveland. As good as they are, their eyes are opened to just how well other Blacks swing the bat, glove hot grounders, and circle the bases. Maybe they could have learned something from watching the Spiders, but the all-Black teams they face are just as good, if not better. For Charles, it is another chance to showcase his skills behind the plate. He guns down four would-be base-stealers during a triple-header.

There are, however, sobering doses of reality for both Charles and Curtis. They begin to understand just how culturally distant they are beyond Wooster's city limits. Henry, whose family has always assimilated within white neighborhoods, understands learning in school is one thing, but educating his kids about an America in which Black men live is something entirely different.

Charles understands this better than Curtis and Joe. His kid brothers haven't experienced the ugliness of hatred and violence that still haunts him. In some respects, his past fuels his future. The fear of failure is a dark place that beckons whenever Charles' confidence is shaken. Football and baseball are his comfort zones.

Catherine, though, isn't expecting either sport to deliver her sons from all that's morally corrupt about America. She demands they find a way to use those games to strengthen their collective voice to send messages far more meaningful than home runs or touchdowns. Henry, for his part, wants his sons to build impregnable self-confidence and unyielding self-worth. His demands are simple: togetherness, forgiveness, loyalty. Even though the Black community is growing in Wooster—albeit at a snail's pace—there isn't yet strength in numbers. It's why Henry and Catherine constantly preach, especially to their sons, to stay close—no matter what distance might separate them. The one thing both parents can agree on: They are not worried about their children drifting apart.

Henry never promises his sons that things will go their own way, but he positions them to have an opportunity to impact the community—and maybe even the country —that turns regularly its back on them.

Even as Major League Baseball owners show no signs of allowing Black baseball players to share the field with their white players, the Follises believe they can make a difference in America's game—or at least to the face of it.

CHAPTER 6

Getting Paid in Shelby: 1902-1903

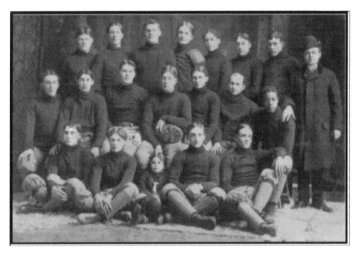

1902 Shelby Athletic Club team photograph.

There is no record of what Follis actually received in dollars and cents for his football services, but it probably added up to an enviable sum—for the turn of the century. —Beacon Magazine (1975)

The Shelby Athletic Club, an amateur football

program, dissolves following the 1901 season. On August 30, 1902, the Shelby *Daily Globe* reports that a committee, led by managers Art Rice and Russell Johnson, has met with the trustees of the athletic association to set up a new arrangement:

> An attempt will also be made to secure Follis, the colored halfback of Wooster. He knows the game and Shelby would like to get a hold of him. There were four or five new candidates for places on the team present last night and there will be an abundance of material on hand for the coming season. Besides, the team will be in better shape than ever before.

> The *Daily Globe* also notes that athletic association trustees will be "required to pay $10 with the treasurer for the purpose of repairing the park and defraying the expenses of bringing the first (professional) team to this city."

The Blues are eager to secure Charles' services. He forces defenses to double-team him, and could thus create opportunities for others like Bill Harris, Fred Tucker, and Joe Cox. When Charles plays defense, his lateral pursuit and speed enable him to cover a lot of territory; when he makes contact there is no hope for the opposing runners.

However, the amateur rules in 1902 are somewhat similar to current NCAA regulations. A key policy prohibits college athletes from playing professional sports; the penalties, like today, include loss of eligibility and amateur status. The same *Daily Globe* piece states: "The rules are the same in all the colleges, in that varsity teams must not schedule a game with any but college teams." Reportedly, Rice, wanting to add Oberlin College to Shelby's 1902 schedule, has failed to reach an agreement with the school. Oberlin's administrators, via correspondence, explain that it is "impossible for Oberlin to meet the Shelby team as the faculty had made a rule prohibiting the college team from playing with athletic association teams."

Days later, Rice is replaced by Frank C. Schiffer, who makes acquiring Charles his top priority. After conferring with trusted associates, including Charles' former Wooster High classmate Dusty Rhoads, Schiffer strings together enough incentives to convince Charles to join Shelby. On September 8, 1902—the year of the first Rose Bowl—the *Daily Globe* breaks the news that Schiffer has "secured Follis the colored player of Wooster. He played with Wooster last season and knows the game thoroughly. He will be a valuable addition to the team and will arrive in Shelby next Sunday."

Of course, the *Daily Globe* buries the lead: The transaction makes Charles the first Black man in America to play professional football. Ultimately, he became the equivalent of a lottery pick. Their agreement includes a salary of $10 per game (around $345 in 2023). In 1902, the average daily wage for a skilled Negro carpenter was around $1.25 per day.)

The Daily Globe buries the lead.

It's unclear whether Schiffer knows or cares about Charles' position on the Wooster College baseball team when he issues the release. He must have realized the announcement would put Charles' eligibility at stake. As it turns out, Charles does not return to Wooster College for the 1903 baseball season.

Schiffer is a crafty businessman. He gives his new superstar running back the superstar treatment from the moment Charles steps off the train in Shelby. He invites Charles over for homecooked meals; he gets Charles a job at Seltzer and Sons hardware store and tailors his hours around football duties; he even finds his star accommodations in an essentially all-white town.

Charles will live on Oak Street in the home of Punkin Johnson, where Charles will soon share a room with old rival Branch Rickey.

There are whispers that Charles' agreement is all under the table, but the funds are real enough for his family back in Wooster. They receive money from Charles all throughout 1902, from his work at Seltzer and Sons and his salary as a football player.

Teams already on the Blues' 1902 schedule are expecting to get paid. The Fremont Crescents even send an open letter to that effect: "You (Shelby) will be expected to pay all expenses for 15 men. Transportation must be at the depot in Monroeville when we arrive there, and we must have our transportation over the electric line here on the (October) 24th ... Hoping that the day will be an ideal one and that your attendance will be large."

Shelby Ohio electric train transportation used by Charles Follis.

Ironically, Schiffer has a difficult time finding a Week One opponent. With Charles Follis in Shelby's backfield, opposing teams are rethinking their approach. Cleveland-area teams claim they'll be more prepared to face Charles by mid-season. Akron North End also punts for a later date as well. Finally, the Akron Planets agree to the date.

For all the anticipation, many on the Shelby roster are skipping practices only days before the season kicks off. Some of Charles' white teammates are still unwilling to share the football with a Black man. To Charles, it's the same ol' racist song. On the other hand, Shelby is different: The 1900 census lists zero people of color (Black or Native American) amongst its inhabitants. One can imagine little has changed by 1902. The Shelby players issue a petty petition to head coach Dr. Morton William Bland; the conflict is resolved only after running back Dave Bushey and right halfback Branch Rickey insist on playing even if it means facing the Planets shorthanded. Bland tells the *Daily Globe* those players who have been skipping practices will realize their mistake "when it is too late," and adds: "If the Shelby team loses the opening game, the interest in the game will be killed on the start."

A fair amount of vitriol is directed toward Schiffer, who has used his financial clout to integrate their town and wield what some consider a personal agenda. Schiffer and Charles both knew to ignore the critics, besides this is nothing new for Charles unlike Schiffer who essentially becomes the Branch Rickey of football by introducing Charles to the world. The bulk of Blues' fans may be calling Charles every off-colored name in the book, but they can't resist buying a ticket for the show.

On an unseasonably hot September afternoon, an edgy crowd of 600 Shelby fans shows up to see the best running back in the country put up mind-blowing numbers. When the Blues take the field for pregame warm-ups, fans can't help but admire Charles. They want to lash out at this Black man, but they also are awestruck by this not-so-mythical figure with supernatural speed.

Though the Akron Planets are considered mild underdogs, many expect their lauded defense to hold Charles in check—but it's checkmate the second time Charles touches the ball.

Sharing the right halfback slot with Rickey, Charles tucks behind his right guard and center, then slips through a crease in the Akron defensive line. A couple of defenders tug at his jersey, and another tries to undercut him as he bounces outside the flying wedge, finds space along the sideline, and leaves the entire Akron defense behind as he races into the endzone.

In a single play, he pushes Rickey down a spot on the depth chart.

Throughout the contest, Bushey wears down the Planets' interior while Charles burns them on the corners for long runs. Charles impacts the game on both sides of the line of scrimmage. There is no stat sheet, but the Planets know what hit them as they lose 27-0. Interestingly, a *Daily Globe* reporter assails the crowd for hurling racial epithets Charles' way throughout the game:

> The most encouraging feature of Saturday's game was the good class of people in evidence along the sidelines, while the disgraceful feature was brought about by the certain few who apparently lost all respect for decency indulged in the most blasphemous yells and indecent remarks. Such actions will have to be suppressed or the patronage of the better class of people will be lost.

But none of the hatemongering slows down Charles. He earns every nickel and dime Schiffer is paying him.

For Charles, the bitter bashing doesn't stop when the whistle blows, but he can't afford to lose focus—not with an impressionable Curtis watching. His now 18-year-old brother is no turn-the-other-cheek type. Curtis is tough, fearless, and he has no qualms with facing down—white men even on their own turf. He's a half-lit stick of dynamite. Like Charles, he's built to play this game.

On a muddy field in Newark, Coach Bland knows he's facing a lesser opponent. His plan appears to include saving Charles for more formidable foes, but Charles isn't one to sit and watch. After all, Henry and Catherine have made the trip together to watch their son play for money for the first time. Nonetheless, there's no need to deploy Charles too much in these conditions. The Blues hammer Newark's defense into submission in the first half, with Charles scoring on runs of 25 and 20 yards. In the second half, Charles anchors the Shelby defense, and Bland's team cruises to a 48-0 victory.

Charles "The Speedy" Follis out races the opponents for a long touchdown run.

While the Blues' second straight shutout isn't much to get excited about, the folks in Newark brave bad weather and slippery footing to perch on nearby rooftops and scale outer fences for a glimpse of Charles Follis. At least on this day, Charles is more significant than the game.

In their third game, the Blues can afford to rest Charles and Bushey against an out-manned, out-muscled Alliance Athletic Club. The Blues wrestle command of the game so quickly, even Coach Bland suits up to play guard. While Shelby empties its bench, Alliance suffers enough injuries that the game is shortened in the second half as they can field only 10 players. Charles punches them in the gut with three long runs that set up three straight touchdowns in a 50-0 rout. Even with Charles out of the middle of the defense, Alliance manages just two first downs.

Finally, the Blues get a chance to test their real level when the Fremont Crescents come into town. The Shelby-Fremont game is the most-anticipated matchup of the season. The Crescents have been carrying a mountainous chip on their shoulder ever since Shelby claimed the title in 1900. It's clear they can't wait to stomp a mudhole in the slightly favored Blues. There isn't just vicious contention between these rival teams. They've talked all week about this being nothing short of a bloodbath—the very kind of game Congress is trying to outlaw.

Everyone with a ticket expects a grueling defensive battle. Charles and Bushey may have had their way with

Alliance, but this cold October afternoon would surely test a ground game that has been steamrolling hapless defenses. The Crescents, however, vow to put up stiff resistance and cripple Shelby's explosive wedge. The *Daily Globe* reports: "It is stated by old football men on the field that this is the fiercest game that Shelby has engaged in this season. The attendance is large and the people are getting their money's worth."

However, as the game unfolds, the Blues camp out in the Fremont endzone, scoring 10 times in 40 minutes—including a beautifully executed 40-yard touchdown run by Charles, who stiff-arms three Fremont defenders as Shelby fans, perhaps hesitantly, cheer him on. Bland then orchestrates a balanced attack in which four players score two touchdowns apiece—including Charles and Bushey. On one spectacular effort, the Crescents lose containment and Charles exploits the vacant corner, then finds another gear along the left sideline before being escorted out of bounds, six yards shy of the goal line.

Charles Follis scores a touchdown in 1902

Bland likes running trick plays out of the V-formation. This time, the crowd is left breathless as Bushey scores on a 62-yard run with an embarrassed Fremont defense wandering aimlessly in search of the ball. This contest is less razzle-dazzle than smash-mouth attack, with Charles delivering short-yardage jabs that take the fight out of Fremont. The final score, 58-0, is reflective of just how much Shelby wanted to snatch out their hearts.

So far, Charles is as good as advertised. It's inevitable that Shelby's remaining opponents will design game plans to take away his big-play capabilities, but ultimately that will require defenders fast enough to shut down the edges. Otherwise, they will have to gamble by loading up the box to stuff the Blues' powerful running game.

East Akron Athletic Club opts to play Shelby late in the season, mostly because they want to devise a scheme to force the Blues to beat them with anyone but Charles. It is a perfectly executed gameplan. Charles, hobbled by a tender knee, carries the football sparingly, and the Blues come spiraling back to earth after dismantling Fremont.

For the first time in his career, Charles plays like a mere mortal—in part because he is managing pain and playing practically on one leg. Though he is stellar on defense (Shelby holds East Akron to just 16 points), the Blues suffer their first defeat of the season.

The Blues' high-powered offense then loses firepower over a three-game stretch in which it scores only 12 points. Charles and Bushey are both banged up, so there is plenty of doubt among the faithful when Shelby faces Lorain Athletic Club—considered a heavy favorite after the Blues' poor performance against East Akron. Nevertheless, Shelby grinds out a gritty 6-0 victory, handing Lorain its first loss in three seasons. When word of the Blues' win reaches Shelby, the entire town celebrates, according to the Shelby *Daily Globe*:

> The news of their victory over the champions of Northern Ohio football soldiers had preceded them by telephone, and before they arrived there was congregated at the Main Street crossing of the Big Four at least a thousand people, men, women, boys and girls and children. Though the hour was midnight and verging on the morning of the Sabbath day, the populace in hilarity cared not a whit.

Defenses dominate the day, but Charles seizes the spotlight. He registers more than a dozen tackles in keeping Lorain's potent offense from reaching the endzone.

At $10 a game, the Blues have made Charles the highest-paid player on the roster. Most players on the roster are making less—far less in some cases, if they're even paid at all. Schiffer probably wants to keep these financial details under wraps. There's a chance that if Charles' salary leaks it could create some problems with other players.

Shelby is among the most successful teams in Ohio, and one of the most financially viable. So, it comes as no surprise when some of their players start to hint they want to be compensated for their efforts. No one is more vocal about his demands than Dave Bushey, whose numbers get a real boost whenever Charles is sidelined due to injury.

Unfortunately, this controversy hinders the team's preparation for a key matchup with the Ohio State University Medics. Disharmony sets in among some players, and a shaky Shelby loses by the same score, 16-0, for the second time in three weeks.

Charles does most of the heavy lifting with some tough, grinding runs between the tackles, but the Medics seal off the end and deny him any chance at breaking off the big gainers that have become the norm. Still, the Medics' coach is quoted as saying: "Shelby's backs are as good as can be found in the state, and with systematic coaching the team would be a strong one."

However, there are rumblings that Shelby's status as a professional team should disqualify them from playing against collegiate programs. According to *The Columbus*

Dispatch:

> In order to be fair, the Shelby team must recognize the fact that they are not competing with university teams on the same basis. No professional dare take part in the university or college teams while Shelby plays four professionals. For the same reason, OMU does not lay claim to the state championship as most of the team is comprised of professional players...The majority of the Shelby enthusiasts can recognize at once the condition the Shelby team would be in if their four professionals—Follis, Bushey, Bill Harris, and [Dubbie] Weiser—were barred from the game.

Amid the disarray, Coach Bland abruptly resigns, partly because the athletic club cannot resolve its financial dispute with Bushey and other players. On November 13, 1902, the *Daily Globe* reports:

> The difficulty was over the matter of compensation for Bushey's services. It seems that Dave Bushey, the Shiloh man who has been playing a star game with the athletic club, felt that he should not be compelled to play the game for absolutely nothing when he was morally certain that the club was making money. For this reason, he demanded some remuneration for his work on the gridiron.

When questioned, Bushey admits that Bland spoke to him but denies that the coach made any suggestions as to his dealings with the club in money matters.

There's nothing to suggest Bushey's demands have come about because he discovers that Charles Follis, a Negro, is pocketing even longer green than anyone imagined. Instead, it appears that Bushey and Charles have developed a pretty good relationship after a somewhat rocky start. The two seem to respect each other's talents, but Shelby's financial future hinges on how well Charles performs. He's the most-feared threat in cleats in the nation. Love him or hate him, he's the draw.

Bushey, a graduate of Wittenberg College, might understand all the business angles, but he's in no mood to make any more concessions. A teacher by trade, he can count the numbers—he has the statistics, now he wants the money. (In 2004, Bushey's son Bob tells the *News Journal*: "Dad made about five dollars a game playing for the Blues. Dad taught history and math, and farmed out here.")

In truth, these problems correspond to Charles' arrival. His presence leads players like Bushey to reevaluate their worth—in part because everyone begins to recognize the value Charles brings to a franchise establishing itself as a dominant force in early professional football. Bushey, by all accounts, deserves a heftier check. Pressing the issue now, though, threatens to derail Shelby's championship run.

In the season finale against underdog Columbus Barracks Soldiers, Charles wants to finish with a flurry. If he can lead the Blues to an impressive win, maybe they'll have a shot to avenge their 16-0 loss to the East Akron Athletic Club.

The Blues play with a sense of urgency for the first time in four weeks and overwhelm the Soldiers. Charles' legs look fresh, and he rushes for well over 300 yards —including a career-best 93-yard touchdown run in the first quarter. As with many of his long, powerful runs, Charles lays out two defenders with his trademark straight arm as he veers away from the wedge.

Shelby sends the Soldiers in retreat, winning 37-0. Again, Charles showcases the skills that prompted Schiffer to seek his services. He excels on defense as well, recording three tackles for losses preventing the Soldiers from getting a sniff of the goal line.

Beyond the numbers, Charles is accomplishing more than he ever imagined, setting in motion the inevitable future of football, which will thrive on the backs of the many Black athletes who will follow Charles through the door he kicked open in Shelby.

1902 Shelby Shelby Athletic Club Football Season Results

Shelby Athletic Club	27	Akron Planets	0
Shelby Athletic Club	48	Newark A. C.	0
Shelby Athletic Club	80	Alliance Orientals	0
Shelby Athletic Club	58	Fremont Crescents	0
Shelby Athletic Club	0	East Akron	16
Shelby Athletic Club	6	Lorain A. C.	0
Shelby Athletic Club	0	Case O. S. U. Medics	16
Shelby Athletic Club	57	Columbus Barracks Soldiers	0
Shelby Athletic Club	226	Opponents	32

Charles Follis leads Shelby in dominating their opponents 226 to 32.

Champions

Beyond Compare. Shelby's Fame In Football Outclasses Every Town In Ohio. Bland's Shelby Champions Annihilate Fremont's Pride Saturday.

89

CHAPTER 7

Tragedy and Triumph

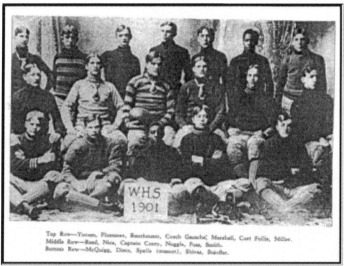

Curtis Follis Wooster High School football team 1901.

An ordinary rebellion in the South American or Central American States is as child's play compared with the destructiveness of the day's game. — An editorial in *The New York Times* on football in the early 20th century Yale Again Triumphant," *New*

York Times, November 25, 1894, News sec.

At the turn of the 20th century, a stunned public is outraged as obituaries of young football players litter newspapers across America. Eventually, editorial boards begin suggesting the sport be outlawed; the *Beaumont Express* even asserts that the "... once athletic sport has degenerated into a contest that for brutality is little better than the gladiatorial combats in the arena in ancient Rome." There are some rumblings from Capitol Hill about the violence in football at every level and how its governing bodies are inept. Indeed, it continues to erode. Finally, Roosevelt defends the sport prior to the 1903 season, telling an audience: "I believe in rough games and in rough sports. I do not feel any particular sympathy for the person who gets battered about a good deal so long as it is not fatal."

A road game at nearby Lorain affords Charles an opportunity to go watch his brothers, Curtis and Joe, play

football at Wooster High School. He has been promising
for weeks that he will make it to a game, but practice and
fatigue have always got in the way. The two-hour ride on
the electric car seemed longer with every trip. Instead of
trying to find a place in Lorain, Charles can even sleep in
the comforts of his old bed on Spink Street. Sometimes,
Charles is concerned with the hard-nosed manner in
which Curtis plays the game. He fears nothing—not cheap
shots at his knees, nor spikes in his back, nor racist slurs
hurled his way. Still, the game takes its toll on Curtis, but
Charles can relate: His body and mind are often battle
weary.

Curtis and Joe are both major contributors for Wooster
High School in both football and baseball. Curtis is a
dazzling halfback with great speed, but he's even better
on defense—using that speed to hem runners in on the
corners. Like Charles, Joe, he excels in the wedge.

At 14, Joe's football career starts amid the shadows
of his brothers. Remarkably, he earns a position in the
starting backfield on the Wooster High School football
team. Like Charles, it doesn't take him long to assume
a leadership role. The coaching staff design plays
specifically with his speed in mind. According to team
captain and quarterback Walter D. Nice:

We used the wedge, and it was murder. Joe was in the
middle, and it was a hard play to stop. (Joe) was just great
and he never complained. He was always ready to do his
part, and a great part of him did. We had a great play that
Joe and I used: I ended up with the ball after a trick pass

to Joe and back to me, and it always went for a good gain, sometimes a touchdown.

In today's game, that play would be considered a double lateral with the halfback (Joe) then faking a run into the line. From the ensuing pileup, Nice could escape for the yardage. Walter Mougey, another former teammate, notes it was known as the "fake buck."

Joe Follis Wooster High School football team 1902.

Charles' younger brothers are carving out a space of their own playing baseball as well. Ultimately, they're even good enough to lock up roster spots on a few Negro League baseball teams. Sports, as Joe and Curtis discovered in the two years after Charles graduated from Wooster, put them front and center in the community. What they do and how they do it matters. They must be more polished, more tolerable, and far more ambitious. According to Charles Follis' niece, Laura Woods Jackson: "My mother would say her daddy had the greatest pride in how his sons conducted themselves even when they were disrespected and mistreated because they were Black. Things haven't always been easy for us in Wooster, but I'm not sure I want to imagine what they suffered." Perhaps Charles' presence inspires his brothers; they both play the games of their lives.

A week later, in the final moments of Wooster High's game, Joe watches in horror as Curtis is attacked by opposing players, who stomp, spike, and maul his brother in full view of 500 fans. The incompetent officials—the very kind the government is targeting—fail to protect Curtis from the "barbarism" football cannot seem to elude as these injuries will not come from sport but rather racism.

Suddenly, the Follises are focused on nursing Curtis back to health as he struggles for his life. The young man who effortlessly weaved through defenses with cat-like agility now is unable to walk, talk and is stricken to the confines of his bed in a coma like state. All that sunshine within him fades amid the stark reality that he'll never play another game. His dreams of playing alongside his big brother are slipping away.

Although Curtis' battle is excruciatingly painful and

difficult, there is a slim glimmer of hope. The family and everyone in Second Baptist Church are praying he recovers. They'll worry about walking and running another time. For now, it's his life that matters most.

Those who govern high school football in Ohio appear to have looked the other way as well. There is no investigation, no review to determine what happened, or —for that matter—any discussion about how to prevent such an attack from happening to another player, Black or white.

In their 18 years in Wooster, the Follises have endured financial hardship, touch-and-go illnesses, racial prejudice, social injustice, false imprisonment, and the emotional trauma of one child's murder—but this atrocity exceeds them all. Compounding matters is the customary challenges of the time: The day-to-day anxieties of raising a Black family in a white community.

Right now, Charles would gladly stand in to take away some of Curtis' pain. He can see into Curtis' dark, sad, brown eyes that life is ebbing with every breath. All he can do, though, is pray that, at daybreak, there's still life in his little brother's body.

It is an awfully tough time for Joe, too. A power halfback built much in the same mode as Charles, he has enjoyed a splendid 1902 season at Wooster High. However, Curtis' injuries are souring him on the game as he relives the traumatic experience of watching his brother be brutally attacked a few feet away. Though he's still willing to put in the work to play when or if Curtis recovers, at some point he stops worrying whether Curtis will play again. He just wants him to pull through so they can fish the waterholes where they find sanctuary from the constant responsibilities of becoming adults long before they could enjoy their childhood.

Sadly, that day never comes. On March 26, Curtis Washington Follis dies "quietly at the home of his parents on North Spink Street," according to his obituary, which also states the findings of the Wooster medical examiner: "The cause of death was catarrh of the stomach, to which, perhaps was added the effect of a severe injury with the high school football team several months ago." (In layman's terms, the beating he suffered on the football field caused inflammation of the mucus membrane in the stomach, causing an increased flow of mucus.).

Curtis W. Follis.

Curtis Washington Follis, (colored)
died last Thursday afternoon, at the
home of his parents on North Spink
street, aged 19 years, 3 months and 15
days. He was born in Cloverdale, Va.,
and came to Wooster about 15 years
ago. When old enough, he began attending the public schools, and at time
of death was a pupil of the High
school, where he was to graduate next
June. The cause of death was catarrh
of the stomach, to which, perhaps, was
added the effect of a severe injury received on the hip while playing with
the High school foot ball team several
months ago. He was a most excellent
and intelligent young man, of best
habits and morals, well esteemed by
schoolmates and all associates by
whom his early death is much lamented. He was a member of the Second
Baptist church. The funeral services
were held Sunday afternoon at the
family residence, conducted by Rev. J.
M. Lockhart, of the Baptist church.
The attendance was large, and tributes
of flowers many. The singing was by
members of the High school senior
class, conducted by Miss Martha A.
Webster. The pall bearers were Louis
Kramer, Harry Schopf, Victor Wilhelm, Durbin Adams, Harry Billiard
and Wellington Webb. Interment in
Wooster cemetery.

The *Mansfield News* details a far more gruesome, targeted, and deliberate act of violence: "A dispatch from Wooster states that Curtis W. Follis, a colored man of that place, died there Thursday as a result of several kicks received in a football game in Mansfield last fall."

Curtis' funeral is held on a rainy afternoon three days

following his death. Reverend J. M. Lockhart delivers an inspiring eulogy, reminding a huge gathering of mourners that Curtis was more than a star athlete: He was a thoughtful young man who possessed an uncanny clarity about life—including the one he lived. Indeed, the closing words of Curtis' obituary read: "He was a most excellent and intelligent young man, of best habits and morals, well esteemed by schoolmates and all associates by whom his early death is much lamented."

As the Wooster High senior class sings to console the family, Catherine and Henry are surprisingly at peace—their son's pain and suffering are finally over.

Joe, on the other hand, is devastated. He struggles with knowing how close he was to Curtis on the field during the attack, and that his efforts to stop them weren't enough to prevent his brother from being mortally injured.

Curtis was much like his brothers. But a great deal separated them, too. His rough edges served as defense mechanisms against a society that he—like his brothers —considered unjust.

The Follis family has always known there were "hits" or death threats placed on the Follis men as Charles experienced an abundance of this and the brothers were no less targeted—Curtis in particular because he was considered the next great in line and mirrored Charles' style of play the most. They will forever see Curtis' slaying as a calculated killing orchestrated and carried out by those who made such threats.

The Curtis Follis episode may not have singularly steered football onto a less violent path, but it may have impacted significant rule changes put in place after the 1903 season.

For one, the "Flying Wedge" formation—the choice formation of the era and one that has been instrumental in all the Follis brothers' success—is blamed for many of the injuries and subsequently banned. Holding penalties became more severe, too: now 20 yards instead of 10.

The Flying Wedge formation

One of the biggest coaching concerns entering the 1903 season is protecting punters, who in the past have suffered career-threatening injuries due to overenthusiastic roughing after the kick. Another development sees more openness about team finances to stimulate more competition. Schiffer, always an innovator, announces that all of the Shelby Blues are now required to sign contracts. Clearly, he'd like to avoid any more in-season conflicts after last season.

Charles isn't focused on either the rules or how much money he is making in his second professional season. He had hoped that his brothers, Joe and Curtis, would someday join him in Shelby's backfield. Curtis' death has a profound effect on the nations premier football player. Charles is making every effort to muster a business-as-usual approach to his conditioning. However, with Curtis gone and Catherine now insisting that Joe refrain from playing football altogether, he finds it difficult to summon enthusiasm before Shelby's season opener against the All-Cleveland Team.

On the eve of the opener, Charles seeks seclusion to mitigate the mental and spiritual tax of the offseason. He settles into a chair on the porch to read the *Daily Globe*. He understands the playbook, which includes many of his own suggestions on formations and blocking schemes. As it was at Wooster High School, he is something of a player-coach, even with A. J. Newcombe filling the actual head-coaching vacancy left by Bland's sudden departure.

The Blues aren't sure they will even have a game until the All-Cleveland caravan motors down Main Street shortly before 2:30 p.m. Some 45 minutes later, both teams hurry through their pregame warm-ups before the 3:15 kickoff.

The Blues stumble out of the gate on their first possession. Then, after holding Cleveland without a first down, Shelby's second possession ends with Bushey tumbling into the endzone to cap an eight-play drive.

Shelby's next possession ends as quickly as it begins. Charles, who has yet to handle the ball, unleashes all his fury on his first carry of the season: An excited crowd of

800 fans is left amazed by Charles' electrifying 70-yard run through Cleveland defenders. According to the *Daily Globe*:

> Follis was sent around left end behind excellent interference with the result that he squeezed in one of his spectacular runs. His interference put the opposing right end and half out of business, and this gave Follis a chance to get up speed, he straight-armed two would-be tacklers and the only one left was Scott, who played defensive full. He was going to be the wise guy and get under that stiff wing. Well, he got under all right. The runner went in the air with the split act stunt that would send the terpsichorean artist to the tall timbers.

Charles may not have foreseen his breath-taking run and the first seen feat of a player hurdling another. Yet, it seems to have an undeniable spiritual connection—a heavenly salute to Curtis, whose last run also covered 70 yards.

Charles unbottles his brute force on the Blues' next possession. Five times he hammers his body into the belly of the Cleveland defense, softening it up for Tucker to run the ball inside the 10 before Bushey's field goal polishes off the 16-0 win.

In their two seasons together in Shelby, Charles and Bushey have had a somewhat indifferent relationship. They are rivals on the same team, mostly because like any good running back desires to be the featured halfback. They split carries somewhat equally, but the spotlight shines brighter on Charles because he is widely considered the best athlete in the game.

Bushey, too, adores the spotlight, not out of arrogance but because he feels he deserves it. Charles just wants the respect of fans, teammates, and foes. He aspires to walk down Main Street without being harassed and to be afforded the dignity to dine with his teammates at a restaurant.

After two years of splitting Shelby's backfield, the two finally become coalesce against Marion, whose defense lacks the manpower to keep Charles in check. Their only recourse is to take him out by any means necessary, so they attempt to injure Charles by spiking him when he is on the ground. Bushey takes exception to the cheap shots. He rushes to Charles' defense. As the *Daily Globe* reports: "Bushey gave the visitor a jab in the same places the chicken got the ax."

Charles never allows himself to get upset over being abused. Even with Curtis still weighing heavily on his mind, it's full speed ahead. He dusts the Marion defense on his second touch of the day as he gathers in a flair pass, sidesteps rhythmically toward the right sideline, and outraces the defense—and his blockers—for a 40-

yard touchdown.

Marion has no answer for Shelby's 1-2 punch of Charles and Bushey. And when the defense again tries to intimidate Charles with another dirty hit late in the second half, Bushey takes up the fight again, this time delivering a sharp elbow to any nearby defender as he recovers his own punt—the first in Shelby's history.

Ultimately, the Blues win going away, 40-0. More importantly, Charles Follis, it seems, finally has won the respect of his influential teammate.

However, Charles soon rediscovers animosity among the whites of Shelby when a few of his neighbors politely ask him to stop frequenting their restaurants. He seems particularly geared up when it comes time to face Branch Rickey-led Ohio Wesleyan University. He's ready to defy anyone who thinks he is less, and he's ready to prove no one can keep him from steamrolling Ohio Wesleyan on both sides of the ball.

Just three minutes into the game, Charles sweeps around the left end for a 25-yard gain to set up a 20-yard touchdown run by Bill Harris. His incredible running game has always stolen attention from his defensive prowess, but Charles is among the best defenders in the game. He uses his strength and uncanny lateral pursuit to stuff the run, and he has the agility and athleticism to cover halfbacks' sideline to sideline. He's a well-schooled, self-taught student of his craft who understands the nuance of defensive strategies. Still, Wesleyan manages to break away from Charles early for a 45-yard gain. Their scouting report must suggest running directly at Charles to minimize his gamut of strengths, but it's shortsighted. Charles blows up the very next play, obliterating three blockers before tossing the halfback for a 10-yard loss.

What separates Charles, too, is his versatility. He's the backfield's best runner, but also Shelby's best open-field blocker—and no one knows like Bushey where his bread is buttered. He tucks behind Charles and squirts through the seams of Marion's defense on a punt return for a 45-yard touchdown." Follis made fine interference on that play from start to finish," notes the *Daily Globe* in its recap. Charles then rips off big runs—35 and 10 yards —on back-to-back possessions before clearing a path for both Harris and Brightman to score on short runs for a 27-0 Shelby lead. Charles, plastered with mud from cleats to shoulder pads, provides another splendid, open-field sprint through the Ohio Wesleyan defense. With Bushey and Dubbie Weiser escorting him through a minefield of angry defenders, Charles turns what looked like a sloppy punch into exquisite 80-yard work of unbridled athleticism.

The Shelby faithful explode after squirming in their seats for three quarters. They feel cheated whenever Charles fails to deliver—and they're feeling like jilted lovers after watching Shelby self-destruct in 1902 and cost their self-proclaimed "home of football" another championship. Of course, they can't blame Charles, who rushed for over 1000 yards, scored 13 touchdowns, and tied for the team lead in tackles while plugging holes all over Bland's roster—runner, kicker, blocker, defender, and on-field assistant coach. One thing is for certain: All 800 fans in attendance want to see the ball in Charles' hands. Like the opposition, they know *that* is when the magic happens.

Ohio Wesleyan's defenders appear to have Charles hemmed in at the point of attack. Bushey chips one defender, then Weiser manhandles another to allow Charles to slip through the gates and high-step along the left sideline. An ambitious Wesleyan defender draws a bead on Charles 35 yards from the goal line. Rather than punish him with the usual stiff arm, Charles jabs into the turf, changes to a gear not seen, then cruises into the endzone, putting the game on ice. A torrential downpour forces officials to call the game with Shelby up 45-0; otherwise, Charles could have enjoyed an even bigger day statistically.

Then the strangest thing happens when Shelby faces the Ohio State Medics on October 24, 1903. Charles begins the game by kicking off instead of Bushey, then commits a rare turnover when he fumbles on his first carry. Weiser can't wrap up the ball, and the Medics come out of the pile still with possession. They score four snaps later to take an 11-0 lead. Charles, Bushey, and Rickey help the Blues march methodically into scoring position, but again the Medics stand firm.

The first gasp of frustration for the Medics' head coach, Riesling, comes when Shelby is awarded a first down after

Shelby coach A. J. Newcombe protests Tucker being held four inches short of the first-down marker. The Blues argue the distance should be measured from the center of the ball instead of the end, and the official, R. C. Skiles —a stockholder of the former Shelby Athletic Association —agrees, thus giving Shelby a first down. An aggrieved Reisling, feeling as if his Medics were homered, elects to forfeit. Here's how the *Daily Globe* reports the chaos:

> Shelby braced up in the second half and held the Medics for downs. Securing the ball, they started toward the Medics' goal, and by fierce bucks and runs succeeded in carrying the ball to the Medics fifteen-yard line, when they were held for downs. Shelby in turn held the Medics for downs and it was Shelby's ball by two inches, the distance being measured by Capt. Howard of the Medics. Angered at losing possession of the pigskin, the Medics refused to finish and were notified before leaving the field that they would forfeit their share of the gate receipts, which amounted to something like $300.

Reisling, infuriated, then goes kicking and screaming himself out of a job. The Blues have received a few gift-wrapped wins over the year, but this 6-0 forfeit victory is something totally unusual.

The Medics, in turn, accuse the Blues of playing a dirty brand of football, earning this retort from the *Daily Globe*: "The truth is that there has never been a team that could best the Medics at that sort of football, and they have a reputation for dirty ball all over the United States. The Medics leaving the field were uncalled for and the coach of the O. S. M. was entirely to blame." The Ohio State Medics' general manager, Mutchmore, agrees. Furious that his head coach might have so sullied standards that they might have to "forfeit the privileges of getting their tuition gratis, Mutchmore fires the Medics' head coach, Reisling.

For one of the few times since he has arrived in Shelby, Charles is held in check against Ohio Northern, whose defense deploys a team of spies to watch his every move. In a very unorthodox move, they place a defender on both ends to contain him within the hash marks. They crowd the line of scrimmage, daring the Blues' other ball carriers—Bushey and Brightman—to step up and deliver before the biggest crowd ever to watch a game in Ada, Ohio. In the blink of an eye, things go from bad to worse for Shelby. Rickey (again moonlighting with the Blues) and Smith Weiser—both of Shelby's ends—are knocked out of the game with injuries. Rickey suffers a season-ending broken leg while Weiser is carried off on a stretcher, unconscious. Charles is excused from the game late in the second half when he suffers a shoulder injury that could sideline him for Shelby's big upcoming game against the Columbus Panhandles. The 125 Shelby fans who have made the trip are left stunned as the short-handed Blues fell 23-0 for their first setback of the season.

In need of a finesse game, the injury-riddled Blues simply can't afford any more bang-ups if they want to keep their title hopes still alive. With Ohio Northern and East Akron also vying for the league championship, the Columbus game is must-win.

Charles, instinctively guarding a sore right shoulder with a slightly torn ligament, returns the opening kick just 10 yards. He takes his time rising from the turf, raising a few nervous eyebrows among the coaching staff. They will happily run Bushey until he drops, but he shows up for the game just before kickoff. Don Tucker, his shoulder also mending, grinds out 10 yards, and Charles gets another 10 as Shelby draws first blood to lead 6-0.

Though the coaching staff probably plans to rest Charles a bit against this underdog opponent, Charles wants to do more after his middling performance against Ohio Northern. After two Tucker fumbles, he gets his chance, running over the Columbus defense for 15 yards to the five-yard line, and the Blues punch it in for their second touchdown. Charles then puts the game to bed with a 27-yard run and a touchdown to give Shelby a 21-5 victory.

Shelby's next matchup, against Lorain, expects to be a tough defensive battle: The Blues have four shutouts, and Lorain's defense surrenders points grudgingly. With that in mind, the Blues sit the ailing Charles, Tucker, and Weiser for the entire first half. It's no secret Schiffer wants his best talent ready for a rematch with Ohio Northern on Thanksgiving Day which could decide the championship. Though takes a while before he can stretch his legs, midway through the third quarter, Charles returns a punt for 30 yards to position Campbell to score as Shelby takes a 7-0 lead. Charles then seals an 11-0 win with the game's longest run from scrimmage—a 30-yard touchdown.

The Blues now themselves jockeying for position to play Ohio Northern for the undisputed championship, but they're not alone. As the *Cleveland Plain Dealer* asserts, "The East Akron Athletic Club football team can justly claim the athletic championship of the state since defeating the crack Ohio Northern university team of Ada, which team a short time ago defeated the Shelby team, who also aspired to the championship. ... The Akron boys were very anxious to meet the Shelby boys anywhere, but they could not be induced to play." Of course, the Blues feel that—with the loss of Charles, Rickey, Weiser, and Bushey—their 23-0 loss to Ohio Northern fails to reflect who they truly are. Shelby launches an aggressive pregame promotional campaign to ensure they'll be recognized as champions if they can avenge their only regular- season defeat:

> The poster reads: Of Athletic Clubs, having defeated every Athletic team they met this season. The result of the Shelby-ONU game at Ada Oct. 31st, was by no means a proof of the relative ability of the two teams, as Shelby lost two of her best men early in the game and the spirit of the remaining players left the field with the injured men. It is the general opinion of those who witnessed the first half of the Ada game that the two teams are very evenly matched, and the result of tomorrow's game will probably be in doubt until

final time is called.

The game will be called promptly at 3'00 o'clock for the benefit of the farmers and visitors who desire to leave town early. Last night a mass meeting was held at the town hall and songs were rehearsed which when heard ringing along the sidelines will stir the Shelby team to its very best efforts, as were the Athenians of old incited on to glorious conquest by enthusing Grecian war songs. A forfeit of $100 has been posted by the Shelby team as a guarantee against the spectators coming on the field during play, and the crowd is requested to bear this in mind.

Music will be furnished by (Edward "Jerry" Smith) Smith's band and the Ada team will bring a band with their rooters who will number about 300. Remember this is the greatest Football event in Shelby's history. Secure your tickets before the game to avoid the rush at the gate. Tickets for sale at both "The Brunswick" and Higgins' Jewelry Store.

At full strength, the Blues believe they can defeat anyone in their league. Their town believes, too, and arrive in droves to watch the lauded matchup.

Shelby Blues team post-game photograph.

The 1903 season has been bittersweet for Charles. His usually rock-hard body is screaming to push the reset button. His ailing shoulder and hips aren't going to heal until the off-season, but mentally he's ready to run through the tape and finish the most challenging season of his burgeoning football career. In reality, the 1903 season—including the championship game—serves to open Charles' eyes to life's priorities. As much as he loves the game, nothing can distract from the loss of Curtis. The pain lingers on deep into the season. He doesn't complain to his teammates, partly because he keeps his distance. Even though he and Bushey are nourishing an awkward friendship, he refuses to drop his guard. The threats, echoes of ugly racist epithets are constant reminders of the hate that claimed his brother's life. On this Thanksgiving Day, he's determined to put forth his best effort. He'll have to play through the obvious pain and mental exhaustion that creeps up on star athletes. At this point, though, Charles is running on empty.

He fumbles the ball twice in the first half, then juggles

a punt before it is scooped up by Bushey. He rips off a run of 32 yards, but again the ball slips from his hands and into those of an Ohio Northern defender. Luckily, the sum of Charles' game is more than running the ball. He helps control the game on defense before he is pulled from the game with Shelby up 21-5. Unfortunately, Massillon defeats East Akron 12-0 to put the State Championship of Ohio, beyond dispute.

Oddly, the same fans who have been harassing him for two years are the very ones who protest when Charles is lifted from the game." Follis played a hard game and the crowd hated to see him benched even though Mayer deserved a try. It was the general opinion that one of the new men and not a regular should have been benched," according to the *Daily Globe*. Charles doesn't complain— the Athletic Club Championship trophy is returning to Shelby.

Bushey and Harris hint at forgoing the 1904 campaign, but Charles promises next season will find him with a body refreshed and spirit reborn—and the memory of Curtis lifting him to greater things than championships.

CHAPTER 8

Follis and Rickey

◆ ◆ ◆

History is sometimes nothing but timing or perhaps it's only his-story.

Charles Follis and Branch Rickey first meet on a baseball diamond in 1901, locking horns as opposing catchers and later that fall on the gridiron, Rickey (Shelby) and Charles (Wooster A.C.). While Charles is just beginning to make a name for himself at Wooster College, Rickey is already a highly touted player for Ohio Wesleyan University, where he would later meet Charles Thomas in 1903—a Black player who becomes Rickey's dormmate. Rickey's relationship with Thomas has been well documented. The film *42* depicts how that relationship would influence Rickey's choice of Jackie Robinson to break Major League Baseball's color barrier in 1947. But the "official" history glosses over the crucial previous crossing of Rickey and Charles Follis, who would leave a lasting impact on the way Rickey would view Black people.

Early on, Follis and Rickey are considered two of the best overall catchers baseball has to offer. The similarities end there, however, when one compares their respective talents. Charles is a power hitter who guns down baserunners with regularity. Rickey is a solid hitter but struggles to thwart steals. In fact, he once surrenders 13 stolen bases in a single game while catching for the St. Louis Browns—an unflattering record that would stand for more than a century. Charles is clearly a cut above, but that does nothing for Black athletes in the early 20th century. Unlike Rickey, Charles will never share a diamond with greats of the day like Nap Lajoie, Christy Mathewson, or Honus Wagner. Though he has the talent and the numbers, Charles also has the wrong skin color.

Charles Follis vs. Branch Rickey

Fate would lead Charles and Rickey to a lily-white patch of rural Ohio, where in 1902 they would become teammates with the Shelby Athletic Association. Prior to this they have always been in opposition in both sports. Locals, predominately segregation-minded, are stunned when they become roommates. Even though he was only a part-time player with Shelby, Rickey becomes something of a confidant. They aren't exactly thick as thieves, but they count on each other when it matters most, on the field. This is where the relationship between Rickey and the two Charles' differ as well as the mentality of both black men he encountered. Where Rickey was in competition with Charles Follis in two sports, which he later loses his position in football and status as Ohio best catcher to Charles in the sports world. Rickey was either a teammate or coach to Thomas so their relationship would've been different in there was no direct nor indirect competing with Thomas as was with Follis. Thomas differs from Charles too, in that he has to be comforted when he has issues with racism. In the example given by Rickey, he recounts consoling Thomas in a hotel room when a sobbing Thomas began to rip at his flesh wishing he could remove the black from his skin to be more accepted by his oppressors. Charles Follis was the opposite and would never look at himself as less than or inferior to anyone. We see how society uses the Charles that best fits their narrative or elevates their heroism by not giving credit to those of color that are successful without a handout or the oppressor taking credit for ones accomplishments. It helps both men are devout Christians and true believers in equality as a birthright. (In fact, in his later years, Rickey would stipulate in his contracts that he would not manage or even be in the ballpark on Sundays—all to honor a promise he made to his mother before signing his first professional playing contract years earlier.) Arguably, those conversations likely lit the fires of inspiration for both.

In the weeks leading up to Shelby's 1903 opener, manager Frank Schiffer has to replace his head coach, Dr. Morton William Bland, who has resigned in the wake of player-salary disputes. Shelby's rivals—Massillon and Akron East End—have upgraded their rosters and, most consequentially, their coaching staffs. Schiffer considers several candidates; then, deciding the best man was already on the club, he offers the job to Rickey.

Even though Rickey suits up only sparingly for the Shelby Athletic Club, he is a valuable member—and already an unofficial assistant coach on the field. More importantly, he is a dependable two-way, multi-position player whose presence on a 15-man roster is invaluable. Rickey also likes the idea of being a "free" player. He has already rejected Schiffer's contract offer to become a full-time member of the team. According to published reports, Rickey has already been "... debarred from 'Big Six' contests last fall (1901) for professionalism." Between moonlighting for two professional football teams and his summer baseball obligations, Rickey has his hands full.

He publicly rejects the Shelby head coaching decision, electing to manage the Ohio Wesleyan baseball team instead. Charles surely understands Rickey's commitment. Both men have been spreading themselves thin, exchanging one ball for another each time the weather changed. As two-sport professional athletes, they must couple training with their routine obligations of family life in the few free weeks they have each year.

When they enter the lineup together for the first time against Marion on October 10, 1903, Rickey—starting at right end—gets an up-close view of the man he's come to admire. He watches as the Marion players take turns trying to spike Charles and force him from the game. Charles never retaliates. He never gloats or shows up the opposition. After the game, Rickey concludes that the Ohio League's only Black player has amazing talent: "Follis is a wonder. And the (Shelby) players are all first class and far above average."

Charles being rejected in Shelby before and after games surely shaped his view of him. Rickey would've witnessed the sheer verbal and physical abuse up close and personal with living with his first Black man. More importantly how this only black man in this profession handled this publicly and behind closed doors. Images of courage, fortitude, bravery and pride in oneself from Charles, no doubt help arm Rickey with the examples of how a Black man can overcome. We see how his approach on Thomas when later faced with opposition would've been directly tied to how his previous encounters were forged as a blueprint of sorts in comforting Thomas.

In the same year Charles loses Curtis, Rickey will suffer an ankle injury that ends his promising career in professional football. His loss has a tremendous impact on the entire team. According to the Shelby *Daily Globe*: "It took the spirit out of them, and the game seemed to go against them." Rickey's injury also effectively signals the end of potentially closer ties between him and Charles, but their brief relationship would have far-reaching consequences.

Charles Follis would become the prototype for all

future football franchises as today teams are still looking for the six foot –200 pound running back with unreal athleticism. Rickey would innovate a management style that would alter not only how baseball approaches fundamentals like scouting, but also its fundamental understanding of humanity.

CHAPTER 9

Complete Player, Incomplete Season: 1904

Charles Follis with 1904 Shelby Blues football team.

The Blues begin the season knowing they have to beef up a little to contend with the physicality of East Akron and Massillon—two bigger, stronger teams that locked horns in the de facto title game the previous season. Shelby has a reputation as a team that relies heavily on execution, but they are a finesse team vulnerable in street fights, as losses to East Akron and the OSU Medics proved in 1903.

Bert Sutter, who has replaced A.J. Newcombe as head coach, has vowed to alter the Blues' persona. They are still lean and fast, but they've pumped up the big men so they're better suited for the inevitable brawls during the championship drive. When push comes to shove, they won't get backed into a corner.

The nagging injuries that kept Charles from playing down the stretch in 1903 are behind him. He has spent part of his off-season working himself into better shape. At first glance, everyone notices he's bigger, stronger.

Charles has been communicating with manager Frank Schiffer by telegram for weeks about the language and figures of a new contract they can both accept. The Blues have had a gentleman's agreement with Charles for the previous two seasons, paying him a relatively handsome amount to commit to Shelby.

A year earlier, Schiffer demanded that everyone sign contracts to avoid any internal strife and petty jealousies among players, many of whom are constantly in a bidding war to negotiate new agreements. As America's first Black professional athlete, no one's value is greater than Charles.

Charles is the Blues' version of a Swiss Army knife. He carries the ball. He is the punter, kickoff specialist, returner and the team's best lead blocker. He is also the team's top returning tackler. Charles is the best football player in the nation. Period. Make no mistake about it, Charles Follis has delivered huge dividends to a once-bankrupt football team that gambled on his talents. The massive crowds came to watch him do his thing. Shelby fans often assail him with racial slurs, but they also voice their displeasure any time he's pulled from a game.

Unlike most of his teammates, Charles understands he has leverage. Marion and Massillon—Shelby's chief rivals—are also vying for his services. He considers an offer from East Akron as well, but their dirty-ball tactics disturb him.

With Dave Bushey leaning toward retirement, the Blues have to return at least half of the Sports most productive ground attack.

Sutter is working to persuade Bushey to play one more season. He's convinced that having Charles and Bushey on the roster will make the offense and defense stronger and put another championship within reach.

The expectations for the Blues are high as they prepare to host Marion Athletic Club in the 1904 season-opening game. The Blues' ground attack gets an extra boost when Bushey decides to return midway through preseason training, but the game will be decided by the team which can best execute its offense on the sloshy, rain-soaked field.

On the opening kickoff, the ball settles at the 35-yard line before Gus Mayer covers it. Marion gets exactly what it expects on first-and-five: a hard-nosed, straightforward run, in which Charles covers seven yards. He turns the left end for eight more before putting Shelby in scoring position with a four-yard punch. Colonel Myers caps the season-opening drive with a three-yard score to give Shelby a 5-0 lead.

After watching both teams get off to a sluggish start, Shelby quickly proves it's the better mudder. Marion has no defense for Charles. Like a skilled strategist in the boxing ring, he continues delivering short jabs that keeps the Marion defense off balance. A 10-yard run here and 15-yard run there leave Marion's defense vulnerable for the knockout punch. With the Blues up 17-0 following a 40-yard score by Weiser, Marion goes down for the count when Charles punches them in the gut with an 83-yard touchdown run. The defense buries the Marion offense dead in its tracks, and the Blues win the season opener, 29-0, to record their 24th shutout in 33 games—a surreal statistic that most everyone takes for granted, even the Blues.

After thrashing Cleveland-based South Brooklyn, Sutter and Schiffer take heat for stacking the home slate with cannon fodder. Criticism mounts when they add (and obliterate) the Akron Imperials—another undersized, inexperienced opponent—to their schedule. Shelby wins both games by a combined score of 101-0.

Schiffer counters the criticism by claiming there are

only three teams in the same class as Shelby—East Akron, Massillon, and Lorain—and then offers East Akron $100 and payment of all expenses to travel to Shelby. The *Daily Globe* opines: "Manager Schiffer is assuming chances of loss in making this offer, but he is willing to do this in order to secure good games."

Schiffer never apologizes for the schedule—at least publicly—but a loss to either of the other three top-tier teams will likely drop the Blues from championship contention.

Charles is dominant in the wins over both South Brooklyn and the Imperials. He scores two touchdowns in each game, including a 71-yard fumble return. Against South Brooklyn, he plays every down on both sides of the ball. If the stat sheets are accurate, Charles averages 12 tackles over the first three games and recovers four fumbles.

In their 3-0 start, the Blues' playbook has established a distinct pattern: Follis runs for 8 … Follis circles the end for 12 … Follis bucks for 4 … Follis goes around end for 7 … Follis nice run for 7 … then Follis sets sail into the open field for a long, game-altering carry that breaks the defense's will.

But Charles wants the ball even more. Sutter runs the numbers through his head. At some point, he'll need to lessen the workload for Charles on offense. He can't rest him much on defense if Shelby expects to pitch a shutout when they host East Akron.

First, the Blues are looking to improve to 4-0 when they travel to Lorain for a rivalry game that grows in intensity every year. Lorain, if only out of pure spite, strikes back no matter the score.

Charles sets the tone early with a couple tough runs between right guard and center. He picks up six yards, then Lorain responds by gang tackling him on his next carry to hold him at the line of scrimmage. Charles stiff-arms two defenders to net seven yards on the next run, but then the drive stalls.

Shelby's defense, with Charles anchoring the middle, is able to stop Lorain on downs. Bushey, Don Tucker, and Follis then gobble up 48 yards to set up the game's first touchdown. Bushey follows the blocks of Fred Tucker to cross the goal line for an extra point to give Shelby a 6-0 lead at the half.

Of course, no Shelby-Lorain game is complete without some form of controversy. The Lorain fans surround the field, partly because there aren't enough seats to accommodate the crowd of 2,500. The fans are warned several times to stay clear, but with Sutter free and clear on an 80-yard scoring run, an overzealous fan staggers onto the field to cut him down.

When Lorain finally does manage to get the ball to the 5-yard line, Charles tosses their halfback on consecutive plays to preserve the team's fourth-straight shutout and a 27-0 win.

In the days after the game, the *Daily Globe* reports, "Manager Schiffer was called upon, and among other things, he said the thing to do now was to get ready to beat Massillon. After this the crowd began to leave, a few at a time, but it was two o'clock in the morning before the street was deserted. All in all, it was a glorious reception which was given to the boys on their return from the field of victory."

Though the Blues rest Charles so he'll be fresh for their upcoming battle with Akron East End, the defense proves impregnable, and Shelby defeats the Deaf Mutes of Columbus, 29-0.

There's no doubt the Blues deserve some criticism for lining up a few easy marks. However, the critics can't argue with Sutter's defense. Led by Charles, it's a collection of hard-hitting renegades whose reputation spreads like wildfire from every corner of Ohio. The Blues' defense will run through walls and knows nothing about finesse.

They begin their preparation for Akron East End knowing their onery defense is the difference between success and failure. Only this time, they'll be facing an Akron team characterized as vicious hoodlums, gangsters, and everything in between. From one end of the roster to the other, Akron players have a take-no-prisoners glare long before boarding the train to Shelby.

Henry, Catherine, and Cora arrive in Shelby early to attend the Akron East End game, the first of two big games—including next week's encounter with Massillon. Charles has called them to let them know it's the one game they can't miss. Though Catherine has vowed to boycott football games since Curtis' death, she finds herself again in Shelby with her pom-poms ready. Joe, still traumatized by his brother's slaying, elects to stay home to rehearse with the Second Baptist Church choir.

Charles strolls confidently into the Shelby Athletic Park with his family and friends in tow. He limbers up his back and stretches the massive muscles in his legs and thighs, firing them up for the upcoming battle against a team the *Daily Globe* has described as "the stiffest team to this city that ever stepped on the gridiron possibly with the exception of the Medics."

The focus once again is on Shelby's Follis-Bushey combo. The Blues make noise early as Charles returns a punt 10 yards, then follows with a 15-yard gain around right end. It's the closest Shelby will come to threatening Akron East End's goal line in the scoreless first half.

The partisan crowd of 2,200 fails to rouse the home team in the second half. Charles runs hard, but meets stiff resistance at both corners. The Akron East End defense locks in on Charles and overwhelms his blockers, continuing a disturbing trend. The offense fumbles the ball away twice, foiling any chances of mounting a scoring drive. Charles dislodges the ball from Akron's halfback in the final minute to keep the game scoreless, and the much-anticipated defensive battle lives up to its billing, ending in a 0-0 tie.

In the final analysis, competing newspapers—the *Daily Globe* and the *Akron Press*—witness two totally different games. Like most media of the time, the publications exhibit unabashed bias. Here's the *Daily Globe*'s perspective of Akron East End: "Every one of them is mighty handy with his fists and most of them are great big double fisted fellows with two or three horsepower behind them. They were mighty anxious to stick their elbow or fist into the ribs of the Shelby squad and a number of times were called for it." From the lens of the *Akron Press*: "When the ball was in Shelby's possession it was advanced by consistent bucking, with an occasional end run by Follis, the colored half. Most of their long gains were made around Akron's right end here the team showed a deplorable weakness. Apart from the dirty playing of the Shelby team, Akron met with good treatment."

Surprisingly, Charles' parents are treated with the utmost respect following the game. It is refreshing for them to see Charles receive a hero's welcome after his stellar play on defense. Still, they now have been shut out five times over the past two seasons—all against bigger, heavier opponents who outmuscle them in the trenches. The gutsy defensive performance has kept the Blues' chances alive. Wins over undefeated Massillon and in their rematch with Lorain could put Shelby in the title conversation.

◆ ◆ ◆

No one has caged the Massillon Tigers this season. They draw from a bigger talent pool and will do—and pay—whatever it takes to establish Massillon as the dominant team in the state.

Schiffer knows he has the best football player in Charles Follis, but his pockets aren't as deep. Even before kickoff on November 6, 1904, there are noisy whispers the Tigers' lineup is scattered with ringers. According to the *Daily Globe*: "Informed this morning by a traveling man that Massillon had a half a dozen ringers in the game and they were the best money could secure. They were gathered up from all over the country, there being one from California and one from Indiana. So it is seen that other teams load up for such games just as well as Shelby."

Schiffer can't complain much; it's not as if he hasn't brought in hired guns, including Charles in 1902. It's just an early form of professional football determining how to structure contractual agreements with players. In fact, the Blues have allocated $300 (of their $400 gate) to bring in two ringers for the Massillon matchup. One is Heifer Resch, who played fullback for Case for two years. He tells The Detroit Free Press Nov, 9 1904, that Massillon is "the best team I've ever played against."

Resch's warning rings true. A crowd of 3,100 watches as the Tigers sprint from the starting blocks and secure bragging rights between the two most dominant teams of the past decade. For the second week in a row, the Blues are blanked by a bigger, heavier squad. Though Charles manages some good power runs, the Massillon defense controls the line of scrimmage, and their back line plugs every hole.

"We simply did not have any chance against them," Resch said about Shelby's 28-0 loss. "I was forced to quit the game with a knee twice its natural size."

A contingent of 600 crestfallen Blues fans board the train for the long ride home.

Of course, this embarrassing loss to Massillon is exactly what the faithful feared when the Blues were facing lesser competition. Tougher games could have exposed many of their weaknesses such as a thin offensive line and a lack of depth on the ends. A better schedule could have given the coaching staff a better idea of how to play their two-way superstar as well.

Ironically, it's Charles' defense and kicking that help the Blues shut out their remaining three opponents—Lorain, Franklin, and Columbus—by a combined score 131-0. The Shelby defense surrenders only 28 points all season—all to ringer-laded Massillon.

CHAPTER 10

Being Black in Shelby

❖ ❖ ❖

In 1975, the Shelby population was 10,000 and not one Black person is listed on the census report." It seems odd for a town which played such a big role in opening athletic doors to Blacks," former mayor Russell Snipes told the Beacon Journal." Except that I guess Shelby has never offered Black people anything they might want or need. Shelby is just a quiet, little town."—Akron Beacon Journal

Whether he's on the road or in his own backyard, Charles cannot escape racist idiots and hatemongering zealots. There is no place to hide, no refuge from all the ugliness, and that further motivates him to lock arms with a growing number of civil-rights activists trying to change, at the minimum, attitudes about Black folks.

Still, Charles can understand the rage fans have against a visiting opponent. The folks in Toledo and

Lorain have a rooting interest in disrespecting him. While he's offended, he's thick-skinned enough to look the other way. The best way to counter that abuse is to jam the football down the throats of the home team.

Billard parlor served as Shelby Blues locker room.

In a 1950 story in the Shelby *Daily Globe*, Burton Brickley, who owned a pool room in Shelby where many of the football players hung out, recalls: "If a team had a star player, the opposition always tried to make sure he did not play the entire game. He would be roughed up. Fractured bones were numerous."

When Shelby visits Toledo on November 29, 1905, it's clear from kickoff that the home team intends to injure Charles. They don't just want him out of the game; they are determined to end his career. Why? The answer is as plain and simple as the scars Toledo players' spikes leave on Charles' back.

Charles is having another career day against the Toledo defense, but he's putting up with more overt kicking, spitting, eye-gauging and biting. Though he's no stranger to the constant barrage of stinging, uncivil commentary, the situation gets so bad that even the *Toledo Evening News-Bee* reports: "Follis, the Shelby halfback, is a Negro and the crowd got after him, advising the local players to put him out of the game."

Apparently, the shouts of "Take the nigger out!" and "Get that nigger!" finally get to Toledo captain Jack Tattersoll, who—having heard enough demented threats to Charles' life—steps into the line of verbal fire.

No one is sure what to expect from Tattersoll. In the past, a couple of Shelby players might intervene—as Dave Bushey has occasionally done to keep Charles focused. Many of the opposing players shared the fans' sentiments. The main difference between the two: Players have the opportunity to act on their hatred with cheap shots and outright dirty tactics.

With Charles jogging back to the huddle, Tattersoll stands near midfield and points toward a few hecklers before gesturing for everyone's attention. The befuddled officials, who have done nothing to calm the storm, watch curiously as Tattersoll screams at the top of his lungs: "Don't call Follis a nigger!" According to the *Toledo*

Evening News-Bee, some in the crowd jeer Tattersoll, but the Toledo player brushes aside both their ignorance and insults."(Charles) is a gentleman and a clean player," he proclaims to the crowd." Please don't call him that." Apparently, Tattersoll is "applauded for his sentiment and the colored player was not molested during the remainder of the game."

Considering the time, a white player publicly protesting the ill treatment of a Black player is remarkable—and it leads one to believe that Charles' character, dignity, and grace were impacting a society infected with racial hatred.

The 1905 Shelby Blues featured black halfback Charles Follis.

Charles surprises his teammates when he practically demands the football. He needs it to hammer out his frustration—as if chopping down a mighty, impregnable oak. Tucking the ball into his left arm Charles sweeps the left end and finds a wall of resistance. He pivots and turns up-field behind two blockers. As four defenders close in, Charles digs his cleats into the turf, then dispenses one would-be tackler with his patented stiff-arm. He then bucks head-on into another defender, who collapses from the violent collision. Suddenly, a path to the endzone forms.

He runs with more than a purpose, intent to distribute his brand of pain to anyone foolish enough to challenge him. For Charles, this outward display of pent-up emotion is his only physical recourse to retaliate. He knew only one remedy, and that was to hammer his nail into the wall of ignorance. Some in the crowd are still shouting obscenities, but it's in vain as Charles torches Toledo with a back-breaking touchdown run that creates a haunting, momentary hush throughout the stadium. Even the Shelby fans are left speechless by the breathtaking display of guile and guts. The Toledo defense spends the rest of the afternoon looking at the back of his jersey.

The Toledo game affirms the mountain Charles must climb to be considered the white man's equal. All the yards he covered, all the touchdowns, all the scars and headaches aren't enough to get him into the good graces of many white fans who shed no tears following the fatal assault on Curtis. Opposing fans have no idea just how much Curtis' death motivates Charles whenever they hurl verbal obscenities or make attempts to physically assault him. He is more determined than ever to allow his greatness to transcend this abuse.

While the game remains a passion, Charles becomes ideologically committed to the lofty ideal that justice will prevail for Blacks. He wants to believe the more than 400 lynchings across the country since he has come to Shelby —including 57 in 1905 and 62 in 1906—aren't reflective of the soul of white Americans. To Charles, Curtis is one of those sobering numbers. His death was just another kind of lynching.

Unfortunately, Charles fights just as hard in the supposedly friendly confines of home. By now, he figures most everyone in Shelby is warming up to him—that they can see beyond his blackness and accept him wearing their team's blue jersey, but this is not the case.

Charles can sometimes be a loner, but he is a member of a family steeped in pride and heritage. He never withdraws from society, and no record exists of him ever resorting to belligerence.

Shelby's reputation as being one of the many "sundown towns," which threatened harm to any Blacks remaining within the town limits come sunset is a constant reminder for Charles. With few exceptions, Charles discovers that many whites are fine with the town's identity, but it's worth the salary he's earning for each game.

Only hours after leading the Blues to victory one chilly November afternoon, Charles is invited by a few teammates to have dinner at a local Shelby establishment. A few moments after being seated, the owners make it clear that Black patrons aren't permitted, declaring: "White football players will be served and can remain, but Blacks cannot." The History of Shelby Football 1894-1985 by Fred Eichinger

Restaurant staff move to escort him from the premises. Charles does not put up a fight. He is far more tolerant than Curtis was; he isn't looking for trouble. He only insists on making a poignant point: a Black man should be allowed to eat at whatever establishment he chooses. He wears a polite smile, which angers the owner further. Charles unscathed by the event takes his items and proceeds to walk alone to his room located on Oak Street. Still, it is another piercing reminder for Charles: Despite all he's done to prove his worth and for the economy of the city, he is "just another nigger" in the eyes of most white folks.

As Charles grows increasingly restless with the falsities of American freedom, he also realizes he now has a spotlight firmly fixed upon him. Nevertheless, as reports of lynchings throughout Ohio, the South and

Southeast, Charles—motivated by big sisters Lelia and Cora—starts to become more outspoken.

There's no doubt sports strengthen the bond between the Follis brothers, but they are far from clones. Joe, who is becoming a standout athlete in his own right, prefers to channel his activism through Second Baptist Church. He uses his considerable influence as a deacon to launch an initiative in which the church takes an aggressive stand to pursue racial equality. He is also active in Wooster community causes, earning a reputation as one of the city's most prolific volunteers.

A towering and commanding figure, Joe relies more on persuasion than hardball politics—a near-perfect copy of his father, Henry. But like Charles, he is known for his lack of compliance. Also like his older brother, Joe's white friends support his work on the playing field but disappear when he renders his thoughts on racial justice. As Charles is captivating the football world, Joe joins local Black leaders in peacefully admonishing President Theodore Roosevelt for his blind eye to poverty and systemic unemployment in the Black community. Neither brother will ever commit to a political party because neither party delivers a platform that adequately addresses the problems facing Black America. Today, Charles might be considered more like Malcolm X—Joe more like Dr. Martin Luther King.

The restaurant incident helps Charles recognize the truth about the business of football: His talents bring bodies flowing through the turnstiles thus generating enormous amounts of money for local businesses from hotels, restaurants, and local saloons. In the games he misses against opponents with winning records, the Blues fall in all but one, and their offense is blanked twice. The Blues need him more than he needs the Blues.

Charles cements his place in Shelby football lore with another great season in 1904, anchoring a defense that registers nine shutouts in 10 games. However, the Blues' albatross is once again a well-balanced (and well-paid) Massillon team. The Tigers devise the perfect gameplan to minimize Charles' speed and effectiveness and dominate the Blues, 28-0.

The Shelby organization is in financial turmoil by 1905 and seek the help from its community to field this year's team. Charles being uncertain of his payments, lends his services to several other teams and vows to return once he can be guaranteed payment. He returns 3 games into the season once his finances are secured. The Blues remain loaded with talent; the only unanswered questions surround a coaching staff who must formulate a gameplan to overcome the menacing Tigers and perennial bully, Akron East End. His body having taken a drubbing from all the punishing runs between the tackles, Charles must adjust how he plays the game, too. The ban of the flying wedge in 1903 may have lengthened his football career, but he does much of the heavy lifting in a season where the Blues again position themselves to contend for a championship. The Blues put together a solid 1905 campaign, but their title hopes are again shot down by a Massillon team that would hand Shelby a 22-0 loss on October 21. Massillon would follow this game with a 58-0 spanking of the Blues the next year to capture one of their five-straight Ohio League championships.

Charles Follis scores.

By 1906, Charles isn't playing a single game without pain. While other running backs are recovering, he's been stretching himself thin each summer playing pro baseball. He even missed some Shelby games in 1906 due to contractual agreements with other teams. When Charles is able to line up against rival Massillon for the season's biggest game, the end seems inevitable as Massillon wins easily 58-0.

He ends up missing half the season with Shelby while honoring contracts to play for other teams. Shelby stays in contention, but the championship is out of reach by the time Charles returns.

Finally, on Thanksgiving Day 1906, as the Blues are playing to a 0-0 tie with the Franklin Athletic Club of Cleveland, Charles suffers a career-threatening injury and is carried from the field by his teammates. Charles decides to tie a bow on a brilliant career that began back in 1899.

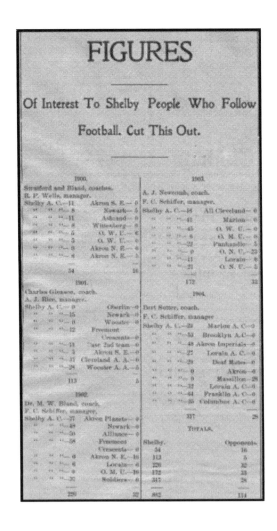

Charles has just enough miles left on his legs and fire in his heart to focus on a professional baseball career. He agrees to sign with the Cuban Giants in New York, where he reestablishes himself as one of the best catchers in the Negro Baseball League.

CHAPTER 11

Charles Follis: Black ~~Cyclone~~ Man

◆ ◆ ◆

We don't think anyone bothered to ask Charles what he thought. The feeling is that some white people were afraid they might like him. And there were Black people who couldn't understand why he kept fighting while others walked away. —Laura Hood Jackson

In the dark of night, with only the faint chirping of crickets to disturb his peace, Charles sits alone on the porch of his parents' home on Spink Street.

The home of Charles Follis and family on 818 Spinks Street, Wooster Ohio.

His world is awash with conflicting emotions as he grapples with the reality of living as a Black man in his time. There's no one with whom to confide in the exclusively white business world where he makes his living—a world that sought to label and contain him. Years of reluctant seclusion have complicated his relationships in places he expects to find comfort and acceptance.

Charles often blames himself for never finding time to raise a family as his father did; to be as deeply rooted in the church as Cora, Joe; or to achieve forgiveness as his mother had, praying that God wash away the sins of the slaveowners who made life an intolerable hell for their family.

With the clock racing toward midnight, he leaps to his feet and walks alone down Spink Street, stopping for a moment to stare at an engine house that's undergoing a facelift. He recalls how it once served as a house of worship for the town's few Black families, a place where they reaffirmed their faith in God and conjured the spiritual strength to confront imminent defeat.

Charles juggles a number of thoughts on the way back home. He's covered plenty in six blocks, none of it about football. There is enough time to consider any future role with Shelby, but he'll focus on his family over the next month. The death of Curtis and disconnect with Jimmy seems to have aged his parents, who again are hoping their seasons of discontent will soon end with Charles' retirement.

Catherine greets Charles upon his return. She touches his soul with a look only a mother can give. He knows what she's thinking—or, at least, he thinks so. Catherine gently puts his head on her shoulders, then whispers, "Show them the man you are."

He kisses his mother, then promises: "I will."

Charles is what his parents emphasized most of all: a caring, respected Black man living a remarkably influential life.

But he wasn't a "Black Cyclone."

The Follis family finds "Black Cyclone" an unflattering moniker. Though the white media apply the title as a salute to Charles' otherworldly athleticism, the nickname shows just how disconnected they are from Black America. What white writers believe to be good-spirited prose, the Follises see as a form of character assassination. To them, it's like calling Charles a "untamed natural disaster." Where were those white writers when Charles jogged five miles from Spink Street to a long stretch of winding road that leads to Apple Creek and other surrounding townships? Could they hear his heart pounding or feel the pain as he gutted out countless wind sprints down dodgy dirt roads through the sprawling cornfields?

Charles himself—as told through the generations—finds the nickname offensive. He never understands why his white teammates are known by their actual names, yet the white media must label him. He associated his name with the valuable thing in his life: family.

Most newspaper accounts insinuate Charles is a quiet, mild-mannered type without a care in the world, or they depict him as a pacifist willing to shoulder a constant onslaught of racist hate. In reality Charles despises the mischaracterization of his persona almost as much as he despises the "Black Cyclone" label. It's counterintuitive for a man trying to bridge the gap between being Black and being an American, as DuBois describes, "in one Black body." He discovers, as the son of a sharecropper, that white folks should not be allowed to define him, what he stands for, and what he's willing to stand up against. In a time where Black people are always forced to adapt, Charles is reluctant to compromise.

However, he is also unequivocally aware of his times. He knows if he pushes too hard there will be repercussions. Of course, the nickname does set Charles apart from the other star athletes of his era with the exception of cyclist Marshall W. Taylor, who is also labeled The Black Cyclone. It's good public relations, and it helps sell tickets. Eventually, he also recognizes its power: The heightened popularity might give him a better platform to push his own agendas—like racial equity.

As Laura Hood Jackson would say years later, "Charles was determined to shake things up."

Eventually, Charles dismantles his fears by becoming a much more in-your-face activist after reading *The Souls of Black Folk* by W. E. B. DuBois, who captivates Charles with this passage: "Herein lie buried many things which I read with patience may show the strange meaning of being Black here at the dawn of the Twentieth Century." Charles is just the man DuBois is seeking as the latter begins building a powerful civil-rights organization—the National Association for the Advancement of Colored People (NAACP). Charles' popularity can be used as a funnel to convey the movement to the masses. He pushes in all his chips after his first meeting with DuBois in

1908. They communicate with each other and exchange a handful of letters over the next year, all encouraging the other to keep up the good fight.

With brother Joe working a diplomatic approach, Charles uses his platform as a well-respected athlete to demand that local and state governments do more to provide job and academic opportunities for Black people. More importantly, he works just as fervently to convince everyone in Wooster—Blacks and whites—to engage in the fight.

The Knights of Pythias an organization of which Charles Follis was a member.

Charles joins many secret Black societies that meet all across the Midwest to discuss growth in Black business, education, laws, and general advancement of the Negro in America. One of those groups would be The Knights of Pythias whom began after a black lodge was denied a charter by the Knights of Pythias' Supreme Lodge meeting in Richmond, Virginia on March 8, 1869. A number of black Americans who had been initiated into the order formed their own Pythian group, the Knights of Pythias of North and South America, Europe, Asia, and Africa. By 1897, the KPNSAEAA had 40,000 members, with Grand Lodges in 20 states and other lodges in the West Indies and Central America. It distributed $60,000 worth of benefits annually and had a woman's auxiliary and uniformed rank as well. His family takes part in local and regional meetings with non-militant groups as well.

Mrs. Henry Follis. Misses Alice, Flora and Lucy Follis Henry Smith, Walter Follis, Frank Newlan and wife and Miss Sarah Sqpall. colored resi dents, went to Silver lake this morning to attend a picnic of True Reformers from all parts of Northern Ohio.

Follis family engaged in Black activism.

Catherine Follis applauds and celebrates how her son's impact on football has lifted his social consciousness, but she is even prouder that he is speaking out against injustices and poverty within the Black community. Henry supports his son's efforts as well. He swells with pride, but—unlike Charles—he's reluctant to thrust himself out front. Nonetheless, he works diligently behind the scenes. Along with Joe, Henry's focus remains in the church. They task themselves with trying to mobilize the congregation and greater community to join their cause.

Charles wants others to join him, so he works hard to recruit other civil-rights activists to help spread DuBois' message throughout Ohio—especially in Wooster, an important passage for the Underground Railroad 30 years before the Civil War. He manages to stay in touch with many of his football and baseball teammates—Black and white—spending long days and nights persuading them to join the fight to help Black souls rise up from their dark past. Charles also finds surprising allies in his former high school and college teammates, who years ago promised him: If he led, they'd follow. However, he worries his white friends might find themselves in more compromising situations than his teammates, especially in Shelby.

People are keeping tabs on Charles, too—especially the Ku Klux Klan, which is intimidating and terrorizing Black families throughout Ohio and across the country, especially those with influence. To exercise social, political, and economic power over African Americans, Klan members utilized violence or threats of violence. KKK members, at times, threatened, injured, and murdered African Americans who attempted to become educated, who tried to vote, who befriended whites, who sought to leave the South, or who sought better paying jobs. In the early 1900's Klans membership begin to sky-rocket across the nation. The Summit County in Ohio boasts of having the largest chapter in the nation with 50,000 plus members during this time period. The family knows that the same policemen who cheer for Charles on gameday would likely offer zero support come sundown.

Charles Walter Follis finds his voice in the fall of 1906. It's a discovery partly influenced by President Theodore Roosevelt, who opts to indulge a growing faction by indirectly sanctioning racism in America.

In a decision that angers Blacks across the country, Roosevelt discharges 167 Black soldiers at Fort Brown in Brownsville, Texas, because he believes they have conspired to cover up the murder of a white civilian following an off-base shooting. Roosevelt ignores the white commanding officer, who claims all of the soldiers were in their barracks when the shooting occurred.

Like an increasing number of Blacks in America, Charles has an uneasy feeling about Roosevelt, the same president who calls whites "the forward race" charged with lifting Blacks to domestic morality. The fact that Roosevelt had to assuage his critics after inviting Booker T. Washington to the White House in 1901 has never sat right with him.

At this point in his athletic career, Charles has developed a heightened political and civil rights awareness that leaves most whites—even those within his circle of trust—feeling somewhat uneasy about his growing activism. They might not want to see him hanged, but they would love to see him silenced. At times, even for the whites who keep slamming doors in his face, Charles can leave room for the benefit of doubt. More than anything, he resents the notion of compromise—and this compels him, along with other activists, to speak out forcefully against Roosevelt's Brownsville decision.

Roosevelt's betrayal of the Black servicemen leaves a deep, irreparable wound in the heart of Black America—and a bitter dose of reality for Charles, who understands no matter how esteemed his accomplishments may be, there will never be a seat at white America's table. He realizes that same America views him as they did his father and grandfather: as overly ambitious Black men whose fate is predicated on the charity of "the forward race." Charles doesn't want any handouts; he has solidified his place in history within a sport and in a city that have each taken exhaustive measures to exclude him. He pushes back against naysayers who judge him by his pedigree rather than his performance.

As of late Charles has been echoing the sentiments of DuBois and William Monroe Trotter—Black lawyers pursuing an aggressive strategy to combat racial discrimination and segregation. They have been leading the Niagara Movement, a Black counter to the "forward race" theory championed by Roosevelt and rampant lynchings across America. Already, Charles and Roosevelt are on opposite sides of the political football.

The Brownsville Affair galvanizes Charles' chaotic emotions just three weeks before his final professional football game on Thanksgiving Day, 1906. He has an epiphany: Grinding out yards on the gridiron and hitting major-league pitching are difficult; achieving the smallest semblance of equality will be far harder. After all, doing those things exceptionally over his entire career has resulted in only more marginalization, ostracization, and dehumanization.

CHAPTER 12

A Lost Era

FOLLIS

Was the Mark in Walk-Over Game.

Local Fans Openly Insulted Wooster Player.-Tried to Spike Him and Called Him a Ni3ger.

On a summer evening in Cleveland in 1909, a bright crescent moon is barely visible beyond the center-field wall. Amid the dim stadium lights, the moon appears to hang on, shining its pale white light over a baseball game that has already stretched five innings beyond the ninth.

In the bottom of the 14th inning, Charles Follis, wearing his baggy gray knickers, proceeds to the batter's box. He swings two 40-ounce bats rhythmically over his broad shoulders, then tosses one into the on-deck circle as if it's a toothpick. He steps out of the batter's box, pulls his red-and-black socks over his scarred knees, and pauses for a moment to glimpse at the fishhook moon.

With two outs, the Star-Light Champs need a baserunner to have any chance of ending this marathon. It is a chance at redemption, too. The Champs lost the opening game of the twilight doubleheader, 3-2, after the Pittsburgh Keystones manufactured a run in the top of the ninth inning to seal the win.

Charles, even with his 6-foot frame still aching slightly from a series of nagging injuries, remains a daunting, imposing figure as he digs into the batter's box. He stares down Pittsburgh's ace, Joe Cross, without blinking. Cross doesn't flinch, either; he stares back, waiting impatiently for Charles to finish limbering up his massive arms over home plate.

--Charles Follis, the well known former Wooster ball player, has donned a uniform again and is playing some great baseball. Follis caught for the Starlight Champs at Cleveland before 8,000 fans Sunday. The Wooster boy also starred with the stick, and made several hits. Follis was the colored catcher for the Wooster Giants and played in several games here.

Orrville Courier May 15, 1908

Thousands of fans came to see Charles Follis display his talents.

A cold, swirling wind blows across Lake Erie, a blistering chill that riles an already frosty Cross. As a misty fog hovers about the stadium, Charles revels in the unadulterated joy of aggravating Cross' usually steely nerves. He remembers how Cross beaned him with a high brush-back pitch when the two faced each other back in 1907. He points to the scar inches below his left eye, then points at Cross, daring him to bring his best blazing, rising fastball.

Everyone fears Cross, a towering, intimidating southpaw who would brush back his mother without offering an apology. Charles can't back down from this challenge. It would be a sign of weakness—an ominous admission that his best days are behind him.

The league's most-feared hitter, Charles is now debilitated playing two professional sports a year for nearly a decade. His bat speed isn't the same. Now, he looks only for the knockout punch—one big, noisy swing. Still, Cross is cautious as Charles steps back into the box, resting his elbows over the inside edge of the plate. He takes two hard cuts before propping his bat on his right shoulder. Cross twice brushes off his catcher before delivering a wicked curveball that surprises Charles and leaves him rocking on his heels.

Cross steps slowly off the mound to think about his next pitch. He wants Charles to think about it, too. Now, it's the same mind game they have played so many times before in helping the Negro Baseball League gain its footing at the turn of the 20th century. Their mental slug fest has become an expected part of their faceoffs.

Again, Charles steps out of the batter's box. He massages his aching left hip while exchanging glances with Cross. If looks could kill, Cross would have been stretched out over the mound, his face buried into the faded red clay. Charles twirls his bat. He digs in, taking two more mighty cuts through the cold night air. Cross slings the resin bag behind the pitching mound before pounding the scuffed ball into his glove. He leans back as if he's reaching deep into Lake Erie, then fires an aimless fastball that comes within inches of Charles' chin. The crowd moans. The Champs protest loudly on the steps of their dugout. The flashback rattles Charles, but he flashes a smile as Cross returns to the rubber like nothing has happened.

Cross shouts: "Get ready. You know what's next."

Charles responds with a steely smile as he waves his bat over the plate after pointing to the outfield fence.

The umpires don't bother to intervene. Negro games are nothing like the wild free-for-alls prevalent in Major League Baseball—a league anchored by supposedly "more disciplined" white players.

Cross fires a fastball that catches the inside corner and only inches from Charles' battered knees. Still, Charles barely moves a muscle. He is willing to take a fastball to the body if it means getting on base.

Charles steps back in the batter's box as he rolls back his sleeves, then digs in. In something Charles never does he barks at Cross in his deep voice, 'Put the ball over the plate so we can go home."

Cross laughs as he circles the mound. He looks into Charles' eyes, daring him to flinch. The Pittsburgh catcher doesn't flash any signs; he, too, knows what Cross wants.

Charles braces himself for the inevitable as Cross reaches back to deliver another tantalizing fastball, a pitch perpetually challenged to find any part of home plate. Only this time Cross leaves the heater belt-high, positioning it perfectly into Charles' wheelhouse. With one thunderous crack of the bat, Charles muscles the ball over the wall in left center to chase home the game-winning run.

Cross doesn't hang his head. Instead, he salutes Charles without acknowledging defeat. Charles doesn't have to boast, either. His slow, joyous jaunt around the bases speaks volumes.

As Charles runs triumphantly toward home plate, Joe Follis sprints from the dugout to embrace the man he most admires. This is what they have talked incessantly about since they were kids and were using splintered two-by-fours to slap balls around uneven fields with cardboard bases.

Catherine and Henry, in attendance, have witnessed Charles' heroics many times before with far more at stake. Yet, even this moment leaves them with an exhilarating sense of pride—in part, because they know these moments will soon be far and few between.

Despite those heroics, the white media largely ignores one of the best games of the year. That, of course, has been the harsh reality of playing in Negro baseball. However, Charles savors some semblance of unfiltered joy against one of the game's best pitchers, and the game-winning hit strokes an ego wounded by the inevitability of age. He lumbers toward the dugout amid the staccato applause of a scant crowd scattered about the ballpark. He tips his hat, then peers almost forgivingly at Cross, who slumps onto the dugout bench with his glove at his feet and his heart still racing from a final tangle with his rival.

Their battles have spilled over from one city, part of traveling all-star contests featuring top Black baseball talent. Though they are prohibited from playing alongside supposedly superior white players, most everyone knows they had big-league credentials. Even in the twilight of their careers, Charles and Cross prove they can still put up a heck of a fight. They prove, too, that Black men could play baseball with equal passion and unparalleled skill.

of Charley Follis—Louden-
ville Paper Champions
the Wooster Player.

The Loudonville Advocate says. A report was circulated Tuesday that Charles Follis, the crack catcher for the Walk-Overs had resigned his position on the team. Although incorrect, the rumor was not entirely without foundation as Mr. Follis was, as he certainly had a right to be, somewhat wrought up over the contemptible way he was referred to in a write up of the 4th of July game as sent in to the Cleveland Plain Dealer, and, in which errors such as the best of professional players occasionally make, were described as dumb playing. This adjective is so uncourteous and harsh in its meaning that it is seldom resorted to by even the most uncouth writer. When the true situation as to the high, esteem in which he was held by every loyal admirer of the game, was explained to Mr. Follis, he naturally took the only sensible view of the case, and passed it up, as a mere incident unworthy of any notice whatever.

Charles Follis displayed his character, not verbally, but by his actions.

Charles has three separate baseball careers—one before, one during, and one after his professional football career—playing for a number of baseball teams in the loosely organized leagues of the day. He even took a trip to Chicago and attempted to get a try-out with the Chicago

White Sox but was turned away at the gate, no doubt due to color.

In his prime, Charles is difficult to pitch around. His bat speed and plate coverage are elite. His eyes are remarkably focused. His swing is free and easy. It has been that way ever since he made his debut with the Wooster Giants in 1900. According to a 1975 piece in *Black Sports*: "Follis's baseball exploits is the talk of the Ohio college circuit as he was credited with many stolen bases, double plays, and even two triple plays in his career, but these skills had to rank second to his reputation as a power hitter." When he turns pro, he takes the Ohio Trolley League by storm and is soon considered the best catcher in professional baseball. He isn't just a prototype —he is a one of a kind, natural-born talent who cultivates his raw skills with the kind of sweat equity few are willing to invest. It's clear that greatness is within reach.

Ultimately, the WAA evolves into the Wooster Giants; with Charles leading them in almost every offensive category, the Giants win the league championship. With the Giants, Charles quickly becomes the most versatile and durable player in the league. No one can match his skill level. He hits with power, but he's just as efficient at beating out a bunt or stealing a base. Charles' reputation as a leader thrust him into the role of team captain, which he embraces, and he becomes one of the most respected figures in the Ohio Trolley League.

He earns a reputation for having the most explosive arm in baseball. He tries his hand at pitching, but thrives behind the plate, where he effortlessly gunned down runners attempting to steal. There is no official number, but some suggest that Charles throws out about 80 percent of would-be base-stealers. Clearly, in the early 1900s, statisticians aren't analyzing every nuance of baseball. Local papers do document feats such as Charles helping to turn two triple plays, or him thwarting five steal attempts—all in a single game. On several occasions, local sportswriters fail when trying to describe his home runs; the routine four-baggers simply "clear the wall."

Then there are, as one writer termed, "the moonshots" that launched into the sky with a thunderous crack. One such moonshot came against the Sebring Amateur Athletic Association on August 20, 1901, at the Wooster fairgrounds. According to the *Wooster Republican* account: "Follis came in for his usual role at bat and knocked out two home runs, one of which went farther than any ball hit at the present diamond. Charles hit the ball so far, so swift that it looked like a pea as it whirled over and across the racetrack." (The racetrack is located about a mile from where the current high school sits today.)

On May 16, 1906, Charles would square off against Herbert Buttons Briggs—one of the best pitchers in the National Leagues for much of the early 1900s. Acquired by Elyria from the Chicago Cubs, the former 20-game winner is projected to be the most dominant pitcher in the Trolley League. Charles reasons no one brings the heat quite like Cross can. He has been waiting for years to face a Major League pitcher—someone deemed out of his league, someone too good to share the same field. Charles tags Briggs for an opposite-field shot that captures the attention of the very scouts who for years have been ignoring him. The ball not only clears the fence, but the parking lot beyond.

With one mighty swing of the bat, Charles does more than hit a home run: He proves that Black baseball players were the real deal. He captures the attention of the sports' elite who have ignored him and other Black players for years. Still, while white scouts take note of his power and prowess, they aren't willing to compromise or relent from their bigotry.

He also would get his money's worth against Herbert Buttons Briggs, notching four hits in six official at-bats.

Charles Follis hits a home run vs Buttons.

◆ ◆ ◆

In 1887, John M. Bright purchases the Giants from Walter Cook. The Giants win back-to-back "colored championships" in 1887 and 1888, becoming the class of the all-Black Middle States League—an independent minor league baseball association that included the Pittsburgh Keystones, New York Gorhams, and Norfolk

165

Red Sox. In 1890, the team becomes the Colored Monarchs of York when they relocate to York, Pennsylvania. A year later, a portion of the Cuban Giants transfer to the rival Gorhams, who are managed by S. K. Govern. In 1896, the Gorhams, bought by E. B. Lamar Jr., become the Cuban *X*-Giants, and persist until the team is disbanded in 1915.

The racist rhetoric toward the tail end of the 19th century is abhorrent. In fact, a *Granville Sentinel* headline, referring to the Giants, reads: "The Darkies Played Nobly," and refers to a Giants pitcher by the name of Gifford "the colored boy." On August 20, 1892, the *Plattsburgh Republican* reports, "The latest news from the field is that perspiration flows freely, and the air is so black with minstrel jokes that the roosters are crowing." As it continues to cement itself as "America's pastime," baseball also becomes a lightning rod for hatred. Still, as the United States population exceeds 75 million, baseball's popularity hits the roof—sometimes for all the wrong reasons. There are eight teams in the big leagues; football, on many levels, is often docile by comparison.

In 1909, Charles is catching for Bright's Cuban Giants, a team long admired for its athleticism. Plus, Granville, New York-area promoters admire the Black baseball team for its ability to draw at the gate.

Charles keeps fighting, hoping eventually more-progressive politicians might allow Blacks into Major League Baseball. Like many other Negro leaguers, Charles is tired of watching white ballplayers with far less talent get paid to play the game he loves.

Predictably, as Charles becomes more involved with civil rights, he faces constant questions about his preparation whenever the Cuban Giants suffer even a minor slump. Not everyone agrees with Charles' aggressive stand on social justice; some of his Cuban Giants teammates warn that he's becoming too visible. Most agree with Charles, but they fear white team owners will find a way to retaliate as they had in the 1890s when they schemed to bankrupt the Negro Baseball League.

Tellingly, even though Charles is one of the most dominant athletes on the planet, the media either fail to interview him or decline to do so—an inexplicable omission best exemplified by this piece from 1909, which describes how Charles was struck by the same bolt of lightning that killed a Cuban Giants teammate.

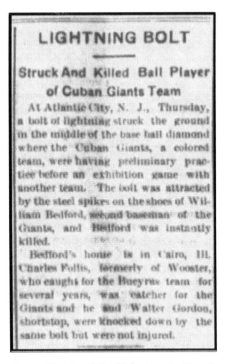

Charles Follis struck by lightning in New Jersey.

As his athletic career is winding down, Charles is becoming far more aware of his desires to be "truly" free and to be respected for the man he has become—not as the "Black Cyclone" or as a ballplayer Americans can keep inside their white lines.

In the spring of 1910, as Charles is contemplating retirement, his friend W. E. B. DuBois is organizing the NAACP. Charles and his family have already done much of the heavy lifting in Wooster, and in many respects inspire part of DuBois' thinking on how to combat racism in America. DuBois wants to unite Black America and galvanize a powerful voice to challenge the racial divide in a country where opportunity itself is increasingly elusive. Over the past few years, Charles and DuBois have discussed everything from the hostile climate in the South to a polarized North, where devout racists with badges and three-piece suits meet Black activism with deadly resistance.

CHAPTER 13

A Legend Cut Short

◆ ◆ ◆

Uncle Charles never compromised his integrity. He never feared anyone. But it seemed like folks were very much afraid of him. —Laura Woods Jackson.

Charles Follis is in high demand, plays as a "ringer" for the Starlight Champs and Loudonville Walk-Overs on the same day.

On April 5, 1910, Charles rolls out of bed on gameday

feeling good about the way he's been swinging the bat. He's felt this way many times over the past couple of seasons playing for the Star-Light Champs of Cleveland and the Cuban Giants of New York, but today's double-header feels different. Now 31, Charles hasn't played without pain since 1905, but he refuses to complain or take games off as so many others do. Besides, the ugly, career-altering injuries to his knees and shoulders are here to stay. After all, football is not the work of a sharecropper. Still, the spike scars all over his body remind him of the lashes covering his father's torso.

He has too much on his plate to worry about nagging injuries anyway: There's the matter of preparing his speeches to the Second Baptist Church and setting up an Akron trip to further the causes of W. E. B. DuBois. Though baseball places great demands on his time and energy, his passion for social justice is beginning to surpass his love of the game. He's spoken to his parents about hanging up his own spikes for good. They pretend to take him seriously, knowing his passion will never allow him to walk away on his own volition.

Since 1907, Charles has been living in Cleveland, where he reconnects with his estranged brother Jimmy after being separated for 21 years. Charles learns that, after becoming a ward the state, Jimmy bounced between foster homes. He moves to Cleveland because he cannot bring himself to reconcile with Henry and wants to protect his own family from the unjust treatment he received in the Wooster legal system.

Charles catches a streetcar to the ballpark on Cleveland's east side. He hopes to arrive two hours before the first pitch so he can stretch and test out some new lumber after breaking one of his favorite bats during the last game.

Charles knows petulant rednecks are going to harass him anytime he leaves his home—by this point, he's long been a target. But that doesn't make things any easier when a gang of white men heading to the stadium recognize him as the "hot-shot colored player" who dominated football for the Shelby Blues. When one of the men suggests Charles stick to football and stay out of politics, he gets concerned.

As the streetcar nears the stadium, the men start littering their commentary with "nigger," among other profanities. Charles brushes off their tirade like he brushes off a Joe Cross high-speed chin pitch. But no matter how many times he tries to look the other way, the comments keep coming. If they were complaining about his game, that'd be one thing—but he knows they don't care about him or his talents.

Perhaps because he's older now, Charles is even more defiant. He refuses to compromise his morals and principles to appease his oppressors. He knows he's come too far. Why soft pedal his resentment of white men who just can't bring themselves to respect him as a human being?

His mind drifts, and he recalls the white store clerk who chased him from the Canton train station decades earlier. Then he thinks of Curtis, who was never afraid to express his feelings or get down in the gutter, roll up his sleeves, and start swinging. Curtis died playing for Wooster High School—a program his older brother created, organized, and once coached. Charles has never been able to forgive himself for being absent when an army of white men attacked his little brother. He was the fighter they all missed. Every run-in with white men since Curtis' violent death adds a log to the fire within Charles—one that is growing harder and harder to contain.

After witnessing lynchings, burnings, and abuse as a child, Charles sees his brother's death among the litany of crimes against Black people. However, he isn't seeking revenge; he's seeking redemption. The entire Follis family regularly attends activist meetings across Ohio, and that catches the attention of their opponents. Charles has been traveling all around the country to communicate with other Black activists, aligning himself with both militant and non-militant groups furthering the Black equality movement. When his visits are made public, his charisma and star power generate a buzz.

Up until recently, militant anti-discrimination-group members have been accompanying Charles on his travels, but he dismisses them on occasion for fear they'll be goaded into more violence. There have been times when Charles has had to get physical, but only to protect himself.

◆ ◆ ◆

Typically, Charles is a first-pitch hitter, gets what he wants in his first at-bat, roping a line drive into the left-field corner for a double. When he races home later to score the go-head run, the scarce crowd musters a soft roar. As he rounds third, the faint chants of loyal fans ease the painful memory of Curtis. The brothers first teamed up only a few blocks away.

It's just after 4:00 p.m. when Charles exits the stadium to catch the streetcar back to Jimmy's home on Norwood Avenue. Again, he's confronted by the same gang of white men. They are agitated by the fact they've been unable all day to get under Charles' skin. But now they're testing his last nerves.

His heart races as he sees where things are headed. Charles searches for an emotional escape route as he tries to keep his cool. He tries to emulate his father, who for years persevered even while white plantation owners conspired to lynch him. But Charles' anger has been surging to the surface ever since that wet winter afternoon in 1903 when white men stole his brother's soul.

As the streetcar winds through downtown and along the Lake Erie shore, a silent Charles readies for the imminent. He considers for a moment how things would go if his brothers—Curtis, Allen, Joe, and Jimmy—were all there to make it a fair fight.

The men attack Charles like a pack of wild dogs, one after another—all determined to put a Black man in his place. He realizes right away that this is no gridiron dustup: These men were out for last blood.

On the curbside of a Cleveland city street alley, still in his dirty uniform, Charles fights for all the past and current Blacks with no chance of winning. He demands these white men respect his willingness to die for what he believes. His refusal to bow down—his *defiance*—increases their anger. Soon, his counterpunches grow less effective, and he's taking more shots than he can deliver.

They pound his body into the concrete, all but lifeless.

Charles' attackers allow him to peel his broken body from the pavement. As he staggers toward his house, his attackers hound him. As he approaches his porch, they deliver a few more damaging blows to the stomach, head, and neck, rendering him unconscious and flee the scene. Neighbors soon discover Charles; he's rushed to Huron Hospital in Ward 9. While the doctors are attending to his grievous injuries, breathing becomes more laborious. Soon, he breathes his last.

Charles Walter Follis life ends the same way it began; fighting to breathe.

◆ ◆ ◆

Charles Follis Death Certificate.

Known to persist unto the 1970s, coroners and medical professionals would over-simplify the deaths of many Black Americans, issuing death certificates without any real investigation. The death of Charles Follis might have appeared straightforward to officials, but there is a knot of loose ends that complicate matters.

The family is concerned with how hurriedly the death certificate is processed, worrying the autopsy was biased and incomplete. For one, the certificate incorrectly states

Charles' date of birth as January 28, 1878 (he was born on February 3, 1879). It also lists his causes of death as asphyxiation as the result of pneumonia. Though Henry signs the certificate without protest, few in the Follis family is convinced Charles could have died from pneumonia. The coroner's report says nothing of the global contusions and severe head injuries, so many in the family believe Charles' "asphyxia" was most likely the result of a collapsed lung suffered in the beating.

Plus, it's too much for the family to believe a 31-year-old world-class athlete could die of pneumonia after playing a double-header in a time when medication was inadequate. Catherine Follis knows better. Family members recall her saying that, although Charles was less than 100 percent, there was no way that he would get up, play baseball, return home, and then *die.*

Although the Follis family vehemently protests and demands an investigation, the Cleveland Police Department performs no inquest. Charles' death is swiftly swept under the proverbial rug, leaving the family with more questions than answers.

The kindling of conspiracy catches a spark when the family considers the suspicious passing of former Cuban Giants manager John M. Bright just a year earlier—one that is never investigated. When he signs Charles, Bright faces some serious threats and backlash for "condoning" Black activism. Whether that played a factor in his mysterious death is still unknown to this day.

Follis Funeral.

The body of Charles Follis, who died at Cleveland Tuesday, will be brought to Wooster on the limited car at 7:15 Wednesday evening. Funeral services will likely be held on Friday from the Follis home on Spink street.

Charles Follis body is transported home to Wooster Ohio.

Charles dies on a Tuesday; his remains are interred on a Friday. The county medical examiner, perhaps deflecting, claims that Henry and Catherine Follis insisted upon a quick burial when they transferred Charles' body to Wooster undertaker Edward E. Boyd. Unable to use most white-run funeral parlors, Black families also hold their viewings and services in their own homes.

From Baptist Church.

The funeral of Charles Follis will be held from the Baptist church corner North Market and Larwill streets Friday afternoon at two o'clock, instead of from the Follis home, as announced Wednesday. It is expected that the services will be largely attended.

Funeral Services for Charles Follis was relocated to the 2nd Baptist Church.

The Follis's original plan to hold Charles' funeral at their home is ruined when the Ku Klux Klan threaten to finish off the Follis men. The family decides to move the standing-room-only services to the Second Baptist Church. Several factions of the Black Knights of Pythias join members of Black militia groups from across Ohio to provide security. (Laura Hood Jackson recalls her mother, Alice—Charles' sister—telling her that it was 46 degrees and sunny on the day of her uncle's funeral. Charles was especially effective in that weather. God, she surmises, must have been a fan.) Following the services, Charles' body is laid to rest on a slanted hilltop beneath a headstone that incorrectly states his birth year as 1880. Myths surrounding Charles' death persist long thereafter. In fact, an article in the *Wooster Daily Record* even claims he "was among victims of the Great Flu Epidemic of 1919."

PAY TRIBUTE TO CHARLES FOLLIS

The funeral of Charles Follis, colored Wooster ball player who died in Cleveland Tuesday, was held from the Baptist church Friday afternoon and was one of the most largely attended funerals held in the city for many months. The spacious auditorium of the church was completely filled, and many friends of the popular young man stood outside while the sad services were in progress. The Mansfield Lodge, Knights of Pythias (colored) was in charge of the services, and a large number of their members were present. The funeral sermon was preached by Rev. H. B. Sworn, pastor of the Second Baptist church, and the minister paid a fine tribute to the splendid life and spoke touchingly of the early death of Mr. Follis. Twenty colored soldiers of Cleveland members of a military company to which the deceased belonged, were here for the services. Interment was made in Wooster cemetery.

Respect and adoration for the Life of Charles W. Follis by many throughout Ohio.

For Henry, the death of his first-born son is reminiscent of other Blacks who died at the hands of callous, cold-hearted white men. One can imagine he just wanted this nightmare to end, Charles being the third of his sons killed by violence. Counting the estrangement from Jimmy, he's lost a fourth, too. Twenty-five years after moving to Ohio from a hostile Virginia, he seeks peace of mind. That might explain why Henry tells a local newspaper that Charles indeed died of pneumonia: "Charles took a shower and then sat down on his porch. He must have sat there a couple hours when he began to shake all over. They rushed him to a hospital, and Charles died there." Henry has never flinched in the face of Klan threats, not even when plantation owners burned his stead and murdered his son. He is a fighter, a survivor, and a family man who has sacrificed his own wants and desires for the sake of his nine children and his wife, above whom he puts no one. But Henry also knows the threats are far from over: Joe, his last remaining son, could easily become a target. Too few people care how Black folks die and the Follis men's bloodline has taken its fair share of losses.

Sadly, shortly after Charles is laid to rest, Henry loses his will to fight and, ultimately, his will to live. Born into slavery, Henry Follis would die at age 65 in the Spink Street home he *owned*. He passes with the heartache of lost sons, but also knowing that he delivered the promise of freedom to his family.

> **Henry. Follis.**
>
> Henry Follis, one of the most highly respected colored residents of Wooster, died at his home on Spink street at 11:30 a. m. Wednesday, after an illness of nearly a year. Death was due to a general break-down. He was 61 years of age.
>
> Mr. Follis came to Wooster from Cloverdale, Virginia, about 25 years ago. He was the father of seven children, one of whom, Charles, the well known ball player, died a few months ago. Six children survive, as follows: James, of Cleveland, Lela, in California, and Cora, Mrs. Peter Woods, Joseph and Lucy, of Wooster. Mr. Follis was a member of the Second Baptist church. Funeral services Friday afternoon at two o'clock.

After losing his 3ʳᵈ son in another tragic death,
Henry Follis dies of a crushed heart.

In the days that follow, the very newspapers that refused to interview Charles—from Cincinnati to Toledo—are the first to laud his contributions to professional sports. One reads: "Follis was a natural hitter and he had an ease about him and a confident smile that always seemed to worry opposing pitchers." Another states: "As a football player and as a baseball player he gained the respect of his associates and opponents as well by his clean tactics and gameness." Though it didn't come in life, one of the finest athletes and gentlemen in American history would get his due respect in death.

Charles Follis established an impregnable legacy for his family, from their roots on Tobacco Road to their lasting influence in Wooster, Ohio. He will be remembered always.

His greatness transcends.

CHAPTER 14

Afterword

◆ ◆ ◆

We had history in Wooster without people recognizing it. We wouldn't need a Black History Month if they put it in a history book. If it was recorded, we wouldn't need to celebrate it. ... No one else can tell your history but you. —Lydia Thompson, Charles Follis' great-grandniece.

Our father, Herman Smith Jr., was a local high school football star. He made sure his sons, from a very young age, learned the sport so we would sit with him and watch games. No excuses. As we grew up, we couldn't go anywhere in Akron without hearing yet another story of our father's blazing speed or how he scored four touchdowns in a game. The adoration of his peers made him an even bigger modern-day hero in our eyes.

On our first-ever organized pee-wee football team, we weren't happy because we didn't get to play on the west side of Akron, where all our friends played. Instead, we had to play on Akron's east side, which seemed like an entirely different state to young kids. On the way to the field one day, I clearly remember—hoping for some words of encouragement—telling my father, "Dad, I want to be just as good as you were."

He was a man of few words, our father. When he did speak, you listened. As we drove to what seemed like Illinois for my first practice, he told me—without turning around—something that would shatter our worldview: "Son, if you think your dad was something, you should've seen your mother's Uncle Charles. He was even better than me."

Our heads exploded. Here was our hero, someone who had the admiration of almost everyone we met, telling us he was so-so compared to some old player we had never seen.

From that day long ago, we wondered: "If Charles was better than Dad, why didn't everyone know about him?"

We spent our summer months in Wooster, Ohio, with our grandparents, Joe and Florence Follis. Unfortunately, Grandpa Joe passed away in 1965, but our grandmother shared their stories with us until her death in 1983.

As a child it was always a delight staying with your grandmother. It was an adjustment living in a city where we may not see anyone who looks like us. In her mind it was a chance to teach and construct young minds to things we weren't accustomed to experiencing in the inner city of Akron. Surely, that's how our Uncle Charles felt when the first members of our family moved to Wooster over 150 years ago.

Family elders and friends, when they'd visit our grandmother, would often make whisper lamentations like, "It's a shame how they did our Charlie," and "Poor Curtis, he never had a chance."

As time passed, Grandma finally told us about the day of Charles' death. She said he was rarely sick, if ever. She recalled Grandpa Joe saying of his fight: his big brother Charles "gave out as much punishment as he received."

History has shown that those who write history shape the future. In our experience, influential biographies and accomplishments of people of color have been shunned by official history, relegated to the realm of familial apocrypha that has been passed down thru generations. Too many times, our history has been penned without much demand for unbiased accuracy when recording major accomplishments, inventions, and events. As a family, we recognize that our grandfathers, Benjamin and Henry, carried the physical scars of their oppressors. Although freed on paper, they were slighted and disrespected because the truth was never told. Most white people want to avoid being associated with their slave-owning ancestors; there is shame in these atrocities, even centuries later. But no matter the span of time between a person and their ancestors, they are family. No one can escape their history. One must acknowledge it, accept it, and move forward to make the present and the future better than the past.

Amid a myriad of tribulations, Charles surged ahead to achieve the kind of greatness that transcends generations. Now, 113 years since his death, there is clarity about his place among accomplished Black Americans who have earned their place in American history.

The problem is, America's history has already been written in stone. Those who have attempted to fabricate Charles' story have also made attempts to keep the family in the dark—to hide the truth. Perhaps they fear the truth will show their history in a negative light.

For these reasons, the story of Charles Follis has been largely dismissed, thus minimizing the contributions of a family who navigated a treacherous path from Antebellum Virginia to become one of the most influential Black families at the turn of the 20th century.

The Follises understood the importance that Charles' life has on the communities of Northeastern Ohio and on America as a whole. What we knew, no one did. When we spoke of him, no one listened. Though we wanted to share his accomplishments and shine light on the atrocities he endured, the media ignored us.

Like other Blacks in America, the Follis family persevered through the atrocities of slavery, the Jim Crow era, the fight for civil rights, and many other unwritten and written laws created to discriminate against people of color. For the first time, this generation possesses the resources and technical tools to expand upon Charles' legacy and share his story with the masses. Others have penned our history with egregious inaccuracies and have been monetizing our Black American story. Now, it is our time to give a voice, to the voiceless.

Charles Follis Foundation.

The Charles Follis Foundation was created to carry on the legacy of Charles W. Follis. Our goal is to protect the Follis family story and to ensure the historical veracity of the Charles Follis narrative.

The Foundation seeks to define Black History on Black terms. This book is part of a larger effort to put Black history in its proper perspective and to shine a light on historical figures such as Charles Follis. Their stories have been largely ignored or highjacked and perverted, to suit the narrative of the author. We want to change this reality. We want to have the truth about the events, accomplishments, and the tragedies of our family clarified and ultimately shared, so others can build and shape a future that is beneficial for themselves and their families.

The Charles Follis Foundation (CFF) has three main

pillars: sports, education, music. The mission is to educate *minds*, inspire *hearts*, and move the *feet* of those in our community by introducing the true stories of courage, strength, and endurance embodied by Charles W. Follis on the playing field and in the real game: life.

We realize that we will never be able to right every wrong or heal every social inequity. Nevertheless, we believe that we can use Charles' example, his character, and the principles of the Follis family to help the lives of marginalized or disenfranchised people realize that their obstacles can be overcome.

It's not a matter of changing society, building businesses, or transforming political and social systems. Social change, unity, achievement, and advancement begins with educating and reaching the heart of one person.

It's The Power Of One.

Joseph & Florence Follis, one flesh.

The power of one is the ability to recognize that one act—one act of kindness, one gesture of appreciation, one civic service, one gift or opportunity extended to those less fortunate, one donation to support a cherished cause, one enrichment of a young person, one moment of supporting the elderly, one instance of sharing your talent, one word of inspiration helping someone to dream beyond their circumstances, one expression of confidence in another— by the power of one—we can overcome any obstacle.

Charles Follis exemplified this with both grace and

greatness. We want our organization to inspire others to share in one act that will help others transcend the adversities, challenges, and despair that they experience in life—one person, one family, one community at a time.

Through the years, the Follis family has emphasized the value of education. It was understood that education was a fundamental component of building and instilling confidence. Education was the vehicle that allowed us to move in various types of social circles. Education was not limited to textbooks, it included faith, observation, and inquiry. Education along with hard work and principled living, would enable the family to achieve success beyond their aspirations.

Our grandfather, Joe—Charles' younger brother—was a living testament to this truth. Though busy with sports, music and church, Joe finds time to fall in love and marry Florence Evans. A Louisiana native of Creole descent. Florence arrives in Wooster in 1909 along with her friend —the daughter of Wooster College President, Dr. Sylvester Scovel.

When she visits the Follis home, Joe is overwhelmed by her grace and intelligence and struck by her pale skin, long flowing hair, piercing dark eyes, and overall beauty. Down the road, Florence attends a service at Second Baptist Church. When his moment arrives, Joe confidently shares his velvety baritone voice with the hopes of swooning Ms. Evans. Their eyes lock: a connection forms as he sings to her—something only they could feel. After the service, Joe reacquaints himself with a simple, "Hello, Ms. Evans. It's mighty fine to see you again."

This meeting kicks off a four-year courtship they would cultivate through letters mailed between Ohio (Joe) and Louisiana (Florence), who would become Mr. and Mrs. Joseph Follis in 1913. The newlyweds start a home in Louisiana, where their first two children, Dorothy and Florence, are born. After a few years, the young family returns to live in Wooster, where they add two more to their family, Alyce and Benjamin—named in honor of Joe's grandfather and uncle (both named Benjamin). In the end, the power of one simple "hello" leads to a loving marriage that lasts over 50 years.

To care for his family, Grandpa Joe worked as a laborer in the College of Wooster Science building. He took every opportunity to learn from the books and the education that was being shared in the classrooms. He would study and perform experiments as if he were a student. He never became a scientist; nor was he published; nor were his experiments used in a major project that advanced humanity. However, he did become a terrific father who motivated his children to value the opportunities a formal education could afford Black people.

1954-Grandpa Joe Follis with grandchildren in Wooster, Ohio.

(Muriel Edwards, Rodney Williams, Sandra Smith, Alan Larkins)

Through the power of one, he took his opportunity to help his family. In fact, all four of Joe's children would receive higher education in college. His three daughters were among the few to graduate and become educators themselves. Joe's sister, Lucy, was considered one of the best future teachers upon graduating from high school in 1907. Unfortunately, the racial climate of the time made this a dream deferred. Fortunately, Lucy's three nieces became the teachers and writers she once aspired to be.

The power of one has had a significant impact on the Follis family. It's a power we all have. If you believe in your own power of one, you can shape your life and make a positive impact on the lives of others—one person, one family, one community at a time.

Our grandfather, Joe Follis, had the responsibility of carrying on the family tradition and name after his brothers' tragic deaths. He spent his formidable days encouraging everyone to pursue an education. Unfortunately, his only son, Benjamin, died in an Army drowning "accident". This accident was no accident, as Benjamin was an excellent swimmer. The truth is, that according to the family, he was disciplined for swimming with white women.

Benjamin Curtis Follis high school yearbook photo

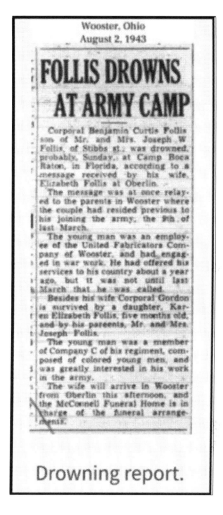

Drowning report.

❖ ❖ ❖

Follis Family love of music.

Music was also an important part of the Follis family. Singing was a way the Follis men and women expressed their feelings and, in many cases, entertained the masses throughout Ohio in the late 1800s to early 1900s. The women in particular, were sought after for many events because of their musical talents and instrumental play, which encompassed all the string instruments.

> Miss Lucy Follis, who has the hono of being the first colored lady, and the second colored student to graduate from the Wooster high school, delighted the audience with a fine vocal solo. Every one was well pleased with her work on Thursday afternoon. She was the only one of the performers who was forced to respond to an encore.

Lucy Follis brings down the house and an encore performance is requested by the crowd.

Merle Alcock a world renowned opera singer
sharpened her skills with the Follis family.

Their musical talents were also displayed in churches, including Second Baptist Church of Wooster. Laura was considered the most talented as she performed in various cities in front of thousands of adoring fans. She was blessed with a rich, pure voice that attracted world-renowned operatic singers like Merle Alcock to perform with her. Alcock's husband, Bechtel, owned a music store in Wooster. His brother, Harry, played on the Wooster High School baseball team with Charles and sang tenor with Grandpa Joe. The Alcocks would spend a considerable amount of time socializing and singing with the Follis family whenever they were in town.

Majestic Opens Tonight.

The Majestic theatre will be op
ned this evening under the manage
ment of Gus Seib. Extensive repair
have been made on the inside, th
entrance being changed entirely. Mov
ng pictures will be shown tonight
and Monday night vaudeville act
will start, to be continued during th
winter.

Miss Lucy Follis has been engag
d to sing and play the piano. Harry
Allis will operate the machine, an
Miss Elpha Brown will preside a
he ticket booth. The appearanc
of the new theatre is very neat, and
hould be well patronized.

*Lucy Follis headlines with her musical talents for
many of Ohio's distinguished class.*

The Follis women were highly talented musicians as
well as excellent cooks being women raised with high
morals and an abundance of self respect. In an interview
of Laura Jackson, she recalled the following when asked
what she did after graduating from Wooster high school:
"When I graduated in June that Fall I went to New
York with Aunt Lucy. I first went to Pennsylvania where
Bechtel Alcock lived. He was married to an Opera singer
(Merle Alcock) and they were good friends with these
people who had all this money - Oh, Charles Schwab, (U.S.
steel industry) - Bechtel Alcock was in the stock market
and a broker with Schwab and had this country place
in Loretta Pennsylvania, and they called and asked Aunt
Lucy if I could come out and work as a "maid"; she as a

cook. So, I left as soon as I graduated and went there and eventually to New York."

Charles and Eurana Schwab

The Follis home was always the nucleus of the music scene in the community. Many of the most talented and popular musicians would come to our family's home to sharpen and hone their skills. It didn't matter the color of their skin, male or female, what mattered was the love of music. Music was a core pillar that gave the Follis family strength, joy, and love to endure any atrocity with blazing hope. From slavery to freedom in a single generation, music held a special place for our family.

As the Follis family exemplified in sports, education, and music, the power of one exists in all of us. The choice is ours. Will we use our power of one, to share in... one act of kindness, one gesture of appreciation, one civic service, one gift or opportunity extended to those less fortunate, one donation to support a cherished cause, one enrichment of a young person, one moment of supporting the elderly, one instance of sharing your talent, one word of inspiration helping someone to dream beyond their circumstances, one expression of confidence in another— by the power of one—we can overcome any obstacle.

We hope this book has inspired you to share your gift with your family and your community. Everything begins with the power of one.

Let your own greatness transcend!

In Honor Of The Follis Family:

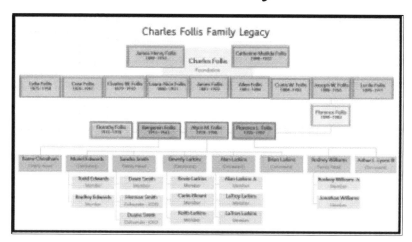

I'd like to express a special "Thank you", to my little big bro, Duane Smith who spearheaded this effort with me to bring our families story to the masses. Bro, your contribution is too expansive to enumerate, but thank you!

We also send a sincere "Thank you", to all the hard-working women, men, institutions, and family members that contributed:

Ralph N. Paulk, Sandra Lee Smith, Muriel Jean Edwards, Karen Cheatham, Rodney Williams, AJ Lyons,

Dawn Smith, Kurtiss Blount, Kevin Larkins, LaTroy Larkins, LaTron Larkins, Todd Edwards, Bradley Edwards.

Wooster College, Wooster High School, Wooster Public Library, The Shelby Museum of History, 2nd Baptist Church of Wooster, Akron Beacon Journal, Orrville Newspapers, Wooster Newspapers, Shelby Newspapers, Mansfield Newspapers, Cleveland Newspapers, Wayne Newspapers, Toledo Newspapers, Pro Football Hall of Fame, Wooster community, Shelby community, the entire state of Ohio.

All those we may have overlooked that have shaped the remembrance of the legacy of our Uncle Charles W. Follis, we thank you!

To Uncle Charles and Uncle Curtis, and Grandpa Joe:

We promised to carry the ball over the goal line for you. I hope we made you proud!

Rest easy, you taught us how to play this game! Thank you!

One Family, One Team, One Goal!

The Power of One!

Charles Follis Foundation

To learn more about the Charles Follis Foundation, please visit us at charlesfollis.org.

◆ ◆ ◆

Charles Walter Follis - First Professional Black Football Player in 1902.

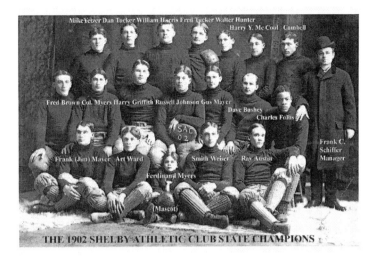

Mike Yetzer Dan Tucker William Harris Fred Tucker Walter Hunter

Harry Y. Mc Cool   Cambell

Fred Brown Col. Myers Harry Griffith Russell Johnson Gus Mayer

Dave Bushey

Charles Follis

Frank C.
Schiffer
Manager

Frank (Jim) Mayer   Art Ward   Smith Weiser   Ray Austin

Ferdinand Myers

(Mascot)

THE 1902 SHELBY ATHLETIC CLUB STATE CHAMPIONS

Shelby

Defeated The Columbus Barracks Football Team By a Score Of 37 To 0. Gridiron Covered With Mud And Snow. Follis Made A 90 Yard Run.

Charles Follis runs for 90-yard touchdown.

1903 Shelby Athletic Club Football Season Results

Shelby Athletic Club	16	All Cleveland All Stars	0
Shelby Athletic Club	41	Marion A. C.	0
Shelby Athletic Club	45	Ohio Wesleyan University	0
Shelby Athletic Club	6	Ohio State Medics	0
Shelby Athletic Club	0	Ohio Northern University	23
Shelby Athletic Club	22	Columbus Panhandles	5
Shelby Athletic Club	11	Lorain A. C.	0
Shelby Athletic Club	21	Ohio Northern University	5
Shelby Athletic Club	162	Opponents	33

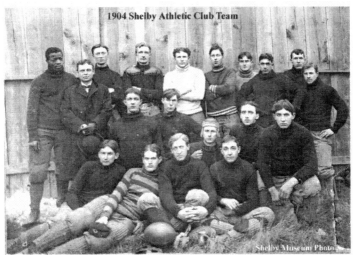

1904 Shelby Athletic Club Team

Shelby Museum Photo

Front row (l-r): Col. Mayer, Ira Stock, unknown, unknown
Second row: Don Tucker, Bill Cook, Dave Bushey, unknown, Gus Mayer
Back row: Charles Follis, Frank Schiffer, Joe Cox, Fred Tucker, unk, unk,
Jones, Claud Simon, Campbell, Bert Sutter

*Charles Follis runs through the wedge to cross
the goal line for another touchdown.*

Base Ball Players to Report.

The following please report at Alcock's music store at 7:30 prompt Tuesday night for the organization of the Outlaw base ball team: —

H. Bricker, F. Zarlengo, E. Snyder, W. Follis, W. Mougey, H. Zarlengo, H. Firestone, J. Massaro, J. Wilhelm, and Harry Alcock.

The Follis family and the Alcock family enjoyed sports and music together.

Charles Follis takes the handoff behind 2 blockers.

A battered and bruised Charles Follis.

Charles "The Speedy" Follis.

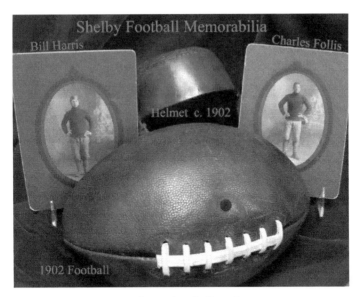

Memorabilia from the Shelby History Museum.

Charles Follis featured as right halfback in Shelby Blues team photograph in 1906..

Spring 1901

*Charles Follis stars as the catcher on the
Wooster College baseball team in 1901.*

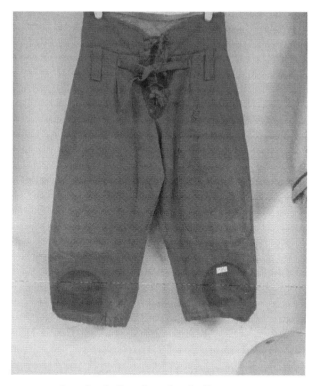

Authentic Shelby Blues football pants, courtesy of the Shelby History Museum.

Opening

Game Of Football Will Be With Marion
Sept. 24. Charles Follis Has Signed For The
Season. Effort Being Made To Secure Dave Bushey.

The outlook for football in Shelby was never brighter than it is this season and with Coach Sutter in charge of the team a successful season is confidently expected by the Shelby athletic association. Games have been scheduled with Marion for Sept. 24, Massillon November 5 and the All Clevelands October 1st. The secretary of the athletic association is now in communication with Reserve college and an effort is being made to get a game scheduled with the Reserve second team. Three practices have already been held and to all appearances the places will all be filled to the satisfaction of the coach. Clark and Moore are two of the new men and they are sure to prove two stars. They are trying for guard or tackle. Both men are stout and quick and will make ideal men in those positions. The position of quarter back will be about the hardest place to fill. Smith Weiser who played this position will not be in the game this year and the place will most likely be given to either G. Mayer or Harry Miller. These two men are now trying for this place. Miller has the advantage as he played this position four years on the team and if he can handle it in his old time form he will make a star at quarter back. McCool and Stock are in the field for center and Moore, Clark, Tucker, Johnson, Cox and Overton are trying for guards and tackles. Coach Sutter, Myers or Miller will be at the ends. The association has secured the services of Charles Follis for this season. The contract has been signed up and football enthusiasts will be pleased to know that Follis will be on the local team again this year. Follis plays half back and there is no better in the state. Every effort is being put forth to secure Dave Bushey and Campbell. If they are secured in addition to the new material Shelby will have a team that cannot be beat. Coach Sutter has already demonstrated that he is fully capable of taking care of the men and rounding them into shape. His years of experience on a college team will be of great benefit to the Shelby team. The association has equipped the basement of the Shifler bowling alley for the use of the team. Shower baths have been placed in and the members of the team will be given a good shower bath and rubbing down after every practice and every game. The team also meets here to recite signals. The opening game will be with Marion, Sep. 24th, and the game will doubtless be well attended by the lovers of football.

*Report of Charles Follis signing his official
professional football contract.*

Family Photo.

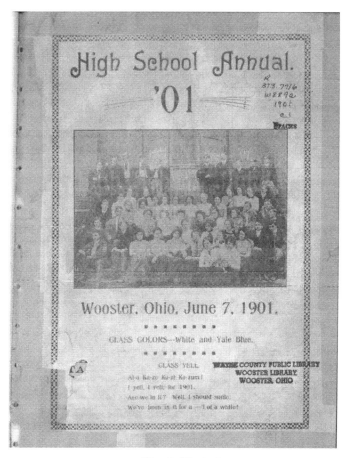

Alice Follis 1901

Lucy Follis (left center) in graduating class of 1908.

Chorus Loses Soloist Follis

WOOSTER — Services for Joseph Follis, 77, of 553 Stibbs st., who died Monday in a nursing home, will be at 2 p. m. Saturday in Second Baptist Church.

A life resident here, he was a deacon of the church, past master of Masonic Lodge 84 and a 35-year employe of the College of Wooster.

Mr. Follis was soloist with the Wooster Men's Chorus and a member of the church choir.

He leaves his wife, Florence; daughters, Mrs. Dorothy Richardson and Mrs. Florence Lyons of Cleveland, and Mrs. Alyce Larkins of Akron; sister, Lucy Follis of Wooster; eight grandchildren, and two great-grandchildren.

Burial will be in Wooster Cemetery.

Friends will be received after 7 p. m. Friday in McIntire Funeral Home.

Joseph Follis Obituary 1965

Florence E. Follis

Florence E. Follis, 93, of Wooster, died Sept. 8 at the Horn Nursing Center.

She was a faithful member of the Second Baptist Church, the Deaconess Board, the Missionary Society, Sunnyside Club, Gold Star Mothers, the Cancer Society, and the Wooster Community Center. She taught Bible classes at Apple Creek Hospital.

She was preceded in death by her husband, Joseph, in 1965; son, Benjamin, in 1943; daughter, Dorothy, in 1978; and grandson, Brian, in 1983. She is survived by two devoted daughters, Alyce M. Larkins of Copley, and Florence L. Lyons of Cleveland; seven grandchildren; 15 great-grandchildren; and two nieces, Alberta Monroe, and Laura Jackson of Wooster.

The family will receive friends at the McIntire Funeral Chapel on W. Larwill St., Wooster, Sunday evening from 7 to 9 p.m. Funeral services will be Monday, 1:30 p.m., at the Second Baptist Church, 245 S. Grant St., Wooster, Rev. Leroy Adams officiating. Contributions may be made to the Organ Fund of Second Baptist Church, or the American Cancer Society.

Florence Evans Follis Obituary 1983

Sandra Smith and Herman Smith, family descendants of Charles Follis stand with Ohio Governor Kasich in 2018, to witness the signing into law February 3rd as 'Charles Follis Day'.

Charles Follis' descendants Todd Edwards, Muriel Edwards and Bradley Edwards celebrate the Ohio marker dedication for Charles W. Follis at Wooster High School.

John Smith a witness to professional football's greatest running backs from 1902-1975, proclaims Charles Follis was the best he's ever seen.

Special "Thank You" to the Shelby Museum and staff. We greatly appreciate the exclusive access and photos shared with this project. To learn more about the history of Shelby, please visit: The

Shelby Museum of History - https://www.shelbyohiomuseum.com/

Sincerely,

Herman D. Smith
Great nephew of Charles W. Follis
Chief Operating Officer
Charles Follis Foundation
https://www.CharlesFollis.org

About the Co-Author:

Ralph N. Paulk is an award-winning journalist whose first book, *Jim O'Brien: Bucking the Odds* was published by Sports Publishing, Inc., in February 2002. The book chronicles the remarkable comeback of a coach who took a dysfunctional Big Ten program and led it to the NCAA Final Four basketball tournament in just two years. O'Brien triumphed over tragedy, particularly the death of his wife, Christine. As a single dad, he taught his craft to his two daughters, both of whom would become coaches.

Paulk, a Michigan State University graduate, has spent more than 30 years as a sports reporter with several newspapers – including Pittsburgh Tribune-Review, Richmond Times Dispatch, Akron Beacon Journal, Detroit Free Press. A native of Ambrose, Ga., he began his career as a military journalist, covering mostly NATO exercises in southern Europe. The award-winning sportswriter was honored as sportswriter of the year in Ohio and Virginia and honored for his investigative and enterprise reporting by the Society of Professional Journalists and Associated Press Sports Editors in three states – including Pennsylvania, where he covered the Pittsburgh Steelers, golf and auto racing.

Paulk, elected in 2017 as president of the largest predominantly Black golf club in the country – Tiretown Golf Club and Tiretown Golf Charities – was a part of the 1994 Pulitzer Prize winning team with the Akron Beacon Journal. Paulk and his wife, Marilyn, have five children — David, Terra, Ralph, Brittany, and Amber.

About the Co-Author:

Herman D. Smith, the great nephew to Charles W. Follis and Grandson to his youngest brother Joseph W. Follis and Florence Follis. Being of direct-blood lineage gives me as the author the authoritative perspective no one else can pen. I have personally heard the stories from my ancestors, witnesses, professional historians, accompanied by family artifacts and Follis enthusiasts alike throughout my lifetime. I lived and slept in the same homes in Wooster Ohio, raised by some of the same family members described in this biography. As children we digested all of our family history, principles and morals, and never before heard factual events we shared with you. These individuals have contributed greatly into shaping me into the man I am today.

Dedicated to my girls Victoria Smith, Alana Smith and Breana Smith.

Made in the USA
Columbia, SC
01 May 2024

c683499e-cb45-4038-b977-5fb758b23b09R01